There will always be a piece missing from my heart, until we are reunited again.

PAGE PUBLISHING
Conneaut Lake, PA

First originally published by Page Publishing 2024

ISBN 979-8-89315-164-0 (pbk)
ISBN 979-8-89315-180-0 (digital)

Printed in the United States of America

PURGATORY MALL

DANNY HILL

Chapter 1

THE COLD AND empty feeling of a concrete cell. Thin blankets and a thin mat to match it. Almost like sleeping on the concrete itself. Shivers constantly being sent down his spine would make Frosty shake. His bones hurt from practically sleeping on metal every night and sitting on it all day long. His body aches from lack of movement, and he's been losing weight from malnutrition. Constant noises all night that prevent from a proper sleep. Random shakedowns all the time because this jail does what they please at any time. A shakedown is when the corrections officers come in and check through your stuff for anything they can find that you're not supposed to have. They leave all your possessions scattered on the floor for you to put back together and put back in a place where they were prior.

That's what it's like in most jails throughout America, and more so in this particular Justice Center, where the word *justice* is used loosely. A jail named a Justice Center is pretty much allowed to do whatever without following a lot of laws pertaining to one's privacy. While most have covers, curtains, or barriers to use while you shower or do your business, this one has none. It's also said that the officers are just as dirty as the inmates that inhabit the cells, but are the inmates really all that dirty? Sometimes the jails and prisons do more harm than good.

Some say they aren't really in the business of corrections but to make people worse. Sometimes people good at heart end up making one mistake and now they're in the justice system, where they are bred and brainwashed into thinking they're bad. This creates more coldhearted criminals in the long run. Maybe that's the design of it all? Instead of rehabilitation, they change you so it keeps the revolving door moving.

Not everyone lets the system change who they are as a person. Some people refuse to allow the system to tell them who they are deep down. That's the case for Bryan Butler. Bryan is a handsome man with brown hair and brown eyes. His skin is pale but has the look of a male model. Bryan Butler is a thirty-year-old who's made many mistakes in his life but only regrets one most of all. The one that got him put into this Justice Center.

A girl Bryan had met in a local bar ended up going home with him. After a great night of drunken sex, she leaves only to tell her parents she was raped when she was asked why she didn't come home that night. Turns out this girl was only seventeen and turns eighteen in two weeks. He also sent her some pictures the morning after she left that her parents had seen as well. Bryan didn't know her age but assumed she was over twenty-one since she was being served drinks at the bar. We all know what happens when we assume though, right?

His bond has been set at two hundred thousand dollars, and he's been locked up for three months already, awaiting his trial and outcome. Locked up in the worst county in the state to be locked up in. Locked up in the worst jail system in the Midwest. Not defined as worst as in how many bad people were there, but worst as in how you live and are treated by the officers.

This justice system treats you like you're an animal that can't be tamed. They have no regard for humiliation or humankind itself. It's almost like they want you to turn bad, so you keep coming back, keeping the revolving door moving. The more people in the jail means more money for the jail coming in from the state. So why not try to make people come back? After all, the money is what pays the corrections officers to keep abusing their power and living their lives just as crooked as the criminals they call animals. It buys their new cruisers and gives them bonuses as well.

Every day they feed the inmates almost stale food with usually already stale bread and desserts. They give them such little amounts that it leaves them hungry an hour after they eat. This forces the ones who don't want to starve to buy snacks and ramen noodles from the commissary. Everybody must get their money though.

They're constantly moving people around to keep them on edge and angry, hoping they act out so they can catch more charges. It's all a part of the plan. The plan is to keep people in longer and keep that revolving door moving. So the news can say what this person did in jail but not say what provoked it, making them seem worse than they really are and inducing fear in the public. Now the public thinks the justice system is doing their jobs and keeping everyone safe, all while creating more anger so when these people get out, they cause more trouble.

Bryan has his own routine, however, that differs from most others. The first few weeks of his incarceration, he slept all day and night, only to get up for meals. Once he got money loaded on his commissary, he bought a drawing pad and notepads and pencils and colored pencils to go with them. So now he decides to sleep all day and still gets up for meals, only to awaken at the last head count of the night. That's when his day really starts. He stays up all night reading and drawing. He does push-ups and sit-ups in between to stay in some sort of shape. He just began writing as he has had some ideas for stories to keep him going while he spends his time in a solitary state.

He writes to his daughter every day so that she knows he never stops thinking about her while he's away. She's not even old enough to read them as she is only a year and a half old. He only writes to her because it makes him feel better, and maybe one day, she can read them and know that he loves her so much. She's a beautiful baby girl named Brenda, who he named himself.

He sits in his cell right now while he hears his block mates yell back and forth to each other after lockdown. They are talking mostly about women and their sex lives, but he knows these guys aren't as smooth as they like to seem. After he writes a letter for his daughter, he prepares his book for a few hours of reading, a nightly ritual. Then he'll do some exercises and some drawing after that.

He waits for everyone to fall asleep. The quiet is what he craves; the silence keeps his mind calm. It helps him focus on his books and the extracurriculars he chooses to do in his cell. The nighttime for Bryan is what the daytime is for everyone else. While he's behind bars, it's what he needs the most to keep his sanity.

He often wonders why he's still in jail as he's not a danger to others nor is he a flight risk. Yet he sits in jail, hoping to get out eventually so he can restart his life. He isn't allowed out on his own recognizance. Even drug dealers are released on their own recognizance, and they are a danger to society, killing people daily with what they sell. At the end of the day, that's how the system works. Let out the people they know will be right back just as quickly and keep the ones in who will follow the rules and law to stay out.

Bryan, by nature, is the hype guy that everyone tends to like. He's easy to get along with and as friendly as they come to. He's someone people can really trust and rely on. He often goes out of his way for people, even when he doesn't really know them, often having it bite him in the butt and break his heart. He's literally the definition of a nice guy or even a romantic. He's always been a sensitive guy that women love to be with, however, most of the women he attracts take advantage of him and leave him feeling worthless. It causes a lot of issues within his own head of not feeling good enough. He believes that it just makes him stronger with every setback he has. His biggest flaw is trusting people too easily, which usually leads to him being let down. In his opinion, jail is the best opportunity to work on himself.

Thinking about his life is another part of his night. Thinking about how to be better while becoming a better person. How to grow and mature into the man he's destined to be. He believes that everything happens for a reason but isn't sure if it's just how the world turns or if there is a God controlling it. As a child, he believed in God and had faith until he reached thirteen years old. He would pray for things that were materialistic or unreal, expecting God to give him his wish like a genie. After so many failed prayers, his faith left him, but deep down, he's always wanted to still believe.

After a good night of reading his book, which right now is *False Memories* by Dean Koontz, and writing a few more chapters of his story, he gets up for the first head count of the day. The corrections officers bring in the breakfast trays, and Bryan grabs his. He eats the jelly off the tray and scoops his cereal into his bowl for later, then drinks his milk and orange juice. Then he lays down on his thin mat and closes his eyes to sleep until they call the head count before lunch.

As he lays there slowly drifting off into sleep, he listens to the quiet of the morning as everyone goes back to sleep after breakfast. He thinks about Brenda and how he feels like he failed her. How he misses her so much and wishes to be with her again. Bryan never truly knew what true love was on his own until she was born. When he first held her, he felt it in his soul. The warm feeling surrounded him as he gazed upon her little face sleeping in his arms. The smile that came to his face that he couldn't remove when he was around her. Oh, how he misses the time they spent together, playing games and music while he sang to her. Always talking to her when she is awake and even while shopping. His attention was always on her when he was around her.

She loved him so as well. She would always watch him and smile at him when he talked. She giggled at him often as he loved to make funny faces at her. When she got a little bigger and started propping herself up on anything she could reach, she would dance with a sway as he sang her songs he liked to listen to. Her favorite was "Hanging by the Moment" by Lifehouse, where she would just stare at him smiling as he sang it. They were great for each other until Bryan made that one mistake and poor judgment call.

Chapter 2

BRYAN OPENS HIS eyes and blinks quickly before wiping the sleep from them. He doesn't feel like he slept at all yet doesn't feel tired at the same time. He sits up and notices he's no longer in his cell. He looks down at his legs and sees he's on his mat with his blanket but his whole surroundings have changed. He looks to his right and sees an officer at a desk, one that he isn't familiar with at all. He looks forward to another officer coming through a door carrying cleaning supplies the inmates use to clean their cells. Then he places the cleaning supplies behind Bryan and walks off.

"Hey!" Bryan shouts at the officer who dropped off the supplies. "Hey, I'm not in my cell."

The officer turns toward Bryan and answers, "Yeah, we're out of room. This is just temporary." And then walks out through another door.

Bryan looks to his left with a dumbfounded face and sees a room nearby. This room has the door open, and he sees a crazy-looking machine. He's never seen this machine before and isn't sure what it is. It is big and futuristic looking.

He then stands up and lets out a huge stretch that made him feel like he was going to grab the ceiling. He glances back to his right at the officer at the desk. The officer is just sitting there reading a magazine, but Bryan can't make out what magazine it is. He then glances around the room and notices the room he woke up in no longer looks the same. It now looks like a small store with racks and items on shelves. It appears to be a sporting goods store with golf clubs and gold accessories. His confusion only lasts merely a few moments before it all feels normal to him.

He walks to the broom the officer dropped off and picks it up. He begins to sweep the floor while he looks at the merchandise on the shelves. He notices the names of the product are just one big blur, and he can't make out what anything says. He shrugs it off and continues to sweep. After a few moments, he looks back at the officer at the desk and says, "Where are my block mates at?"

The officer looks up from his magazine and says, "They're around. I think they're next door or something." Then he looks back down at his magazine that seems far too interesting.

Bryan begins sweeping the floor again and then sees a women walk past him and enters the room with the weird, crazy-looking machine. She appears to be in space gear but without the helmet. He walks to the door and listens in on the people now standing with the women. "All right, our next simulation will soon begin. I'm going to have the officer buzz in our next class," she says then walks out past Bryan to the desk. "Would you be able to buzz in my class please?"

The officer looks back up from his magazine and replies, "Sure thing, doll." Then he hits a button, which makes the door behind him buzz and unlock. The class walks out, and the lady walks them back into the room with the crazy machine.

Bryan begins to think to himself, *Simulation? Like a space simulation? At the jailhouse?* He keeps glancing into the room at the machine and at the people gathering around as he continues to sweep the floor at the same time. He now notices more and more people are walking through the store as if they're shopping. He looks back at his mat and blanket that are still there, but nobody seems to notice them there at all. He looks down at his clothes and sees he's still in his orange jumpsuit and nobody is alarmed by that either.

Suddenly, a golf ball rolls up to his feet and hits his jail shoes. He bends down and picks it up. He looks in the direction where it came and sees two older men with big baskets full of golf balls. It now looks like the room is a driving range for golfers to work on their swing indoors.

"You can keep that!" one old man yells over at Bryan.

The other turns toward Bryan and slaps his ball so that it rolls to his feet as well. "Have that one too!" the other old man yells.

"Thanks," Bryan says as he bends over to pick that one up too. He looks at both golf balls in one hand and sees one is white and the other is yellow. Both look monogrammed, but the words on them are all blurred out as if he isn't supposed to read them. He puts both golf balls in his pocket and continues to sweep the floor.

This feels weird but at the same time it feels normal, he thinks to himself as he sweeps the floor. Then the feeling of it being weird goes away, and it all just feels like every day in the jailhouse. He looks to the officer at the desk and asks, "What time is it anyway?"

The officer glances from his magazine and looks confused. "Time? What's time?"

Bryan shakes his head in disbelief. "Where's the clock at?" he asks.

The officer answers, "Clock? What's a clock?" Then he goes back to reading his magazine.

"What the hell is going on?" Bryan says as he looks around the room and then notices there is an office behind the officer at the desk now. It has two women and a man behind a huge desk with scientist outfits on. All three are just typing nonstop. He looks back to his mat and sees it's still there and realizes it is the only thing that hasn't changed since he woke up.

It's all beginning to feel like a dream, but he feels so awake at the same time. Kind of like an out-of-body experience, but he's sure he's not asleep. He looks back at the room with the machine and sees a bunch of people in space suits gathered around it closely. He thinks, *How cool would it be to join that. Get a feel for space. Maybe I'll join the simulation.* He begins to walk to the room, and then what feels like a glitch happens. The whole room blurs, and Bryan rubs his eyes. It didn't help because he still saw blurring in the room.

Then he hears people talking around him but sees no one. They're talking as if they're with family out for a day of shopping and just hanging out. Then he hears kids screaming and turns himself toward the screams.

He sees three little boys in between a crowd of people playing catch with a small football. The scene he had around him has changed again. He sees they're running through a food court in what seems to be a mall. "Right here!" one boy yells as he then catches the ball.

"I'm open!" another boy yells as he then catches the ball.

The third boy yells, "Me! Me now!" But the football overthrows the little boy and goes right to Bryan who catches it with his fast reflexes. The third boy says, "Throw it here, mister." Bryan pump fakes it then throws it to the little boy.

The boys keep moving, and Bryan moves with them as they take turns throwing the ball back and forth to one another. Bryan catches it again and, instead of throwing it to one of the boys, decides to pause. He now has a strange feeling brewing inside of him. He's almost frozen in time right along with everyone around him except for the little boys. One boy runs over to Bryan and asks, "Are you okay, mister?"

Bryan looks down at the boy and asks, "Where are we?"

The boy laughs and answers, "You know. Now throw me the ball." He runs through the people as if he's running a route, and Bryan tosses the ball deep into him. He catches the football like a great wide receiver catching a touchdown pass, and the boys disappear into the crowd of people. As soon as they disappear, the crowd of people begins moving again as if they were never frozen at all.

You know? Bryan thinks to himself. *What's that supposed to mean?* Bryan stands in place, frozen in thought, thinking about those words the little boy said to him.

"You know?" he says aloud. "Do I really though?" he questions himself.

He begins to walk through the crowd and quickly realizes that nobody notices he's there. Nobody acknowledges him as they brush past him so closely. He begins to feel like a ghost but hasn't seen anyone pass through him yet. The weird feeling begins to overwhelm him again, but as fast as it comes on, it leaves just as quickly.

He continues to walk until he reaches what feels like the center and spins around slowly looking at the scenery. He notices he's in the middle of a food court, but he can't make out any of the names of the restaurants. They are all blurred out like everything else that should have words. He looks upward and sees that the mall has three stories to it. He now sees stairs that lead all over. It reminds him of the crazy stairs painting he's seen many times in movies and shows.

It all looks as confusing as everything else has been so far. He finally sees a path leading up to the second floor and instinctively begins to walk to it. He walks up the stairs unsure of where it really leads, but he has this feeling like it's where he's supposed to go. He just feels it in his stomach, and his legs just automatically take him up.

There are now fewer people walking suddenly. He sees at the top of the stairs a group of girls standing and taking what looks like prom pictures. The girls are all huddled together smiling and hunched over facing the camera. The camera is held by another girl, but she is a blur to him. He can't make out what she looks like but just sees a silhouette of her body and the camera. The girls that are hunched over remain still as if they're frozen and can't move. Bryan walks up the stairs to the top and passes them, looking at them as he goes by. After he gets past them, he turns back around and sees them all facing him just staring blankly. They stare at him like they're robots that are ready to kill at any moment.

He turns and continues walking a bit before turning back to them, only to notice they're now gone. The crowd is now back in action, moving around him and past him as if he isn't there at all. He finds himself moving through the crowd again like a ghost moving through walls with ease. He sees all these stores around him but still can't make out what they say. He looks down at his clothes and sees he's now in jeans and a white T-shirt instead of his orange jumpsuit like before. He pauses and stares at his new threads. Faded blue jeans and a pair of Adidas shoes.

When did this happen? he thinks as he holds his arms out.

At that moment, he hears a chime go off and looks up to see a woman watching him through the crowd. He can't make out what she looks like, but her presence feels so familiar to him. Her whole face is a blur. After he feels like they have locked eyes, she begins to walk away through the crowd and vanishes among the people. He yells, "Hey!" but just silence comes out of his mouth.

He begins to run after her in hopes of catching up. "Hey! Wait!" he yells, but again silence comes out of his mouth. All he can hear is the chatter of the crowds of people around him, but he can't make out what any of them are saying. It's all mumbled together and sounds like a stadium of crazy fans cheering and booing. He continues to follow where the woman went but can't locate her at all. The feeling of her presence now vanished, and this sense of comfort had now gone.

He hears a man's voice yell out of nowhere, "All right people, stay with the tour!" The scenery around him changes once again, and he's now standing next to a spiral staircase. "Hey! I said stay with the tour!" the man yells at Bryan.

Chapter 3

LONG SCRAWNY FINGERS come from behind Bryan and grab his shoulder, turning him at the same time. Bryan looks and sees a tall, gangly-looking man standing in front of a group of about seven people. All the people on the tour are carrying cameras as if they are on vacation at a great attraction. The tall gangly man looks more like a security guard by the way he's dressed. Bryan looks at his shoulder, which still contains the man's long scrawny fingers, and brushes them off. "Don't touch me!" Bryan shouts at the man.

The tall gangly man, still looking at Bryan, says, "Stay with the tour." He goes to grab Bryan's shoulder again, but Bryan sidesteps his advance.

"I said don't touch me!" Bryan yells again at the man. The man then turns and guides the group of seven up the spiral staircase. "I'm not a part of the tour!" he yells at the tour. "I'm just a prisoner!" Despite what he said, his feet begin to move up the spiral stairs as if he has no control of them at all. "But I'm just a prisoner," he says again. Then he gives up fighting it and lets his feet take him away.

He follows as the tour of seven moves up the spiral stairs that are now following the tall gangly guide. There is no talking of any kind, just a man leading them all. Bryan sees the stairs and people, but their faces are blurry like everything else. *What's going on? Am I in a dream? Or is this some sort of weird memory?* he thinks to himself.

As they reach the top, the whole place blurs out, including the people and the tall gangly guide. The mall reappears but with more stairs surrounding him now. People are walking everywhere, but now it seems like he's in a mall hallway than in the mall itself with the stores. Bryan looks around in a panic and begins to wonder if he's losing his mind. Then he thinks, *Have I already lost it?*

He walks over to the railing and looks over only to see hundreds of stairs surrounding the bottom and what looks like hundreds of hallways filled with thousands of people just walking aimlessly. The feeling of being sick overwhelms Bryan, but the urge to throw up just lingers as if he physically can't. It all starts to spin around and around and then Bryan falls backward. He lands on his butt and closes his eyes, now just listening to all the voices of the people talking. Their voices just mesh like one loud echo. He puts his hands over his ears and squeezes his eyes together to where he only sees black and some colors spiraling around. He takes his hands off his ears and now hears just silence. He opens his eyes slowly, allowing his vision to unblur, only to see people once again moving past him. Slowly, their voices begin to fade back in. It's just normal now—not loud but tolerable.

Bryan sits on the floor while he looks around at all the people. He notices that none of them care he's on the floor. None of them even notice he's there, just walking past him and over him at times. They walk over him without disturbing him or themselves in one swift motion. At this point, he begins to feel like he doesn't exist. Like he's dead, and it's his spirit that never left earth. *Is this what ghosts feel like?* he thinks to himself as he begins to feel lonely and out of place all together. *Am I doomed to walk the earth like this? Is this my fate? Is this my hell?* he thinks as he looks around at the topsy-turvy stairs and people that don't notice him.

He slowly stands up and goes back to the railing to look down from it. He finds that he's looking down from the second floor, and all the hallways and stairs below him have now disappeared. He sees that he's back in front of the food court despite being on another floor. He sees people sitting, enjoying meals, and others walking around with shopping bags. He thinks to himself, *Maybe me being an inmate was the dream. I just don't know anymore. Everything feels so real yet so fake at the same time.*

He just wants to get back to his mat now. Just to lay down and go back to sleep, just so he can see if he will wake back up in reality. He doesn't know where to even go to get back to his mat, nor does he see a way to get back to the first floor. He sees stairs that lead to a third floor but none that go back to the first floor. Out of his left ear, he hears a chime go off. The chime sounds a second time, and Bryan instinctively looks to his left toward where the soft tone came from.

The tone itself sounds like a wind chime blowing in a subtle breeze. It almost makes him feel calm and hypnotic in a way. He gets this sensation of being a child once again. Living at his parents' house in the country, listening to the wind blow, and chimes ring in the breeze. The smell of summer rain is setting in, and the feeling of humidity dropping as the clouds get darker and settle in their wicked-looking ways.

Through the crowd of people, he sees that woman yet again, standing beside a storefront with chimes above her head. Another clink of the chimes goes off one more time, and then she walks into the store, disappearing as soon as he steps in. Bryan begins to rush over to the store, moving past the people with ease. As he moves toward the store, the crowd of people gets thicker and thicker. He begins to use his hands and arms to push people. As he does, he realizes quickly that he doesn't feel anyone or anything.

He makes it to the store and stops to read it, but it's blurred out. He thinks about how he didn't feel the people, and then realizes he hasn't felt a thing since arriving at this place. The cleaning supplies, the golf balls, or even the gangly man's hand on his shoulder. Nothing has he felt since arriving. Bryan begins to push people as they walk past him. They continue walking as if he never touched them at all. Unbothered by his shoves like it's just another day for them. He doesn't feel anything, skin or clothes, as if none of this is real. *I can't feel anything at all, like I'm numb to everything*, he thinks to himself as he stares down at his hands with his fingers spread apart.

He knows something isn't right, and now he feels like the woman has something to do with it. He looks up at the doorway and takes a deep breath as he steps through the threshold. His eyes are now closed, and his face is scrunched, hoping that it would take him somewhere familiar.

He opens his eyes after stepping through and sees black. Just pitch black like all lights were cut off. He turns back around but sees no light from where he came. Just more pitch-black darkness surrounding him. The sound of wind rushing past him begins to pick up and intensify. It brushes through his hair and past his face. The cool breeze feels nice and gives him goosebumps on his arms. The hair on his arms is standing straight up as if they were magnetized to the wind, forcing its way past his body. It's the first thing he's felt since leaving his jail cell and arrived at this godforsaken place. He can't help but relish it and enjoy the stimulation he's receiving.

His body begins to spin around with the wind, and he gets the feeling that he's falling, but he isn't quite sure if he's doing that either. Just then, there are flashes of colored glitter around him. Red, green, and orange flicker in no particular pattern. Now yellow and blue join the mix and flash faster and faster, almost making him feel disoriented. He closes his eyes and lets out a scream, and as he does, it all stops.

Chapter 4

HE OPENS HIS eyes and sees the outside. He sees an underpass with a gas station on the other side of it. He stares calmly at the gas station that appears to be vacant. Abandoned for years like it's been all but forgotten. The underpass hasn't been maintained in a long time either. Grass and weeds are overgrown throughout it. He's standing at the edge of the underpass ready to walk in and get to the other side.

He begins walking, and after a few steps, he stops suddenly. His walk is interrupted by the swing of a saw blade attached to a rope. It comes from the wall and swings past him. He steps back and observes the blade, and it swings back and forth until it reaches its stop. Bryan then looks up at the walls of the underpass and notices more blades attached to ropes just ready to swing toward him as he moves. "Booby traps," he says aloud.

He observes another saw blade like the first and then what looks like a long handsaw blade after that. The handsaw blade is super long and thin, with a lot of bend to it. He turns around to go back but a wall has appeared now closing him in. His only way out is forward. He looks down to the ground and studies the moist vegetation-filled floor for any triggers for the booby traps. He notices one spot that appears to be fake, and so he steps a foot on it and then jumps back quickly. The second saw blade swung from the wall past him like the first one. He watches the blade go back and forth multiple times before coming to a stop, dangling from the middle of the ceiling of the underpass.

He begins to move past it while watching the blade. He sees it barely swinging and spinning in one place. After he got past the blade, he takes a few more cautious steps and then stops. He's now close to the handsaw blade on the wall and knows the trap must be nearby. He observes the ground once again and sees a patch like the other and knows that must be the trigger. He prepares himself to stomp on it. He examines the wall one last time and then stomps hard before quickly moving back a few steps. He watches as the blade releases from the wall and swings fiercely past him. This one is swinging more than the rest in an unpredictable way. He sees it turn sideways as it appears that it will strike him with this swing. Bryan closes his eyes and takes a deep breath as he hears it whoosh past him and get stuck in the wall on the other side.

He opens his eyes and looks to the right where the blade is now stable in the wall. He lets out a huge sigh of relief but then feels his upper body slowly begin to slide. He looks down at his legs and notices his upper body is sliding right off them. His upper body completely slides off and hits the ground, making a gruesome splash onto the damp vegetation below. He reaches for his intestines and all his innards and begins to attempt to put them back in. With all his efforts, they don't stay and continue to slide out of him. He looks up to his lower body, which is still standing there in place. Slowly, he sees his lower body start to fall on him. It hits him and covers him up to where all he sees is pitch black once again.

The sound of his own breathing echoes around him. He hears the drip of water falling about every three seconds. The sound of his breathing becomes faster and heavier, but he isn't breathing at all. The drips now become faster and faster as if it's a torture method to make him talk. It's now torturing his senses. He has the feeling like he's standing straight up now but can't see past the pitch-black darkness. The water drips have stopped, and silence surrounds his senses. The silence lasts about five seconds before the sound of heavy wind picks up and brushes past him. It makes him feel like he's inside a tornado. He begins to hear a sinister laugh through the wind that reminds him of the Wicked Witch of the East laughing during the tornado in *The Wizard of Oz.* This laugh, however, sounds more sinister and eviler, like a demon.

He begins to spin in a whirlwind of air as if it's carrying him around. The laugh is now getting louder and louder, stronger and stronger. Then it's as if the world crashed down upon him, and he slams into the dark black ground below. He crashes like he's been forced into the earth straight to the core.

Silence. Nothing but undisturbed silence all around him. He opens his eyes slowly and sees light seep through his eyelids. He opens them and blinks a few times, seeing blurred light all around him. Not blurred like the faces or words, but blurred like he just closed his eyes and pushed on them for a minute, causing a blurred vision. He's lying on his stomach and brings his hands to his chest, pushing himself up to his knees. He blinks a few more times to regain his full vision and sees a red figure walking toward him.

"Wow! You just crashed through my ceiling!" the red figure says to Bryan. "You could've knocked first, and I would've said just comemit." The red figure begins laughing that same laugh Bryan heard while in the tornado of air. "Do you get it, Bryan? Comet! It's a play on words." The red figure laughs even harder.

"I'm sorry, sir. I couldn't control where I landed," Bryan says back with sympathy. He finally regains his full vision and looks up at the red figure. He sees a red man in a red suit, but instead of a human head, he has the head of a bull. Instead of human legs, they're the hind legs of a horse. "Are you the devil?"

The red figure laughs some more and answers, "You can call me Lucifer, or Satan if you wish. I do prefer Lucifer if we're being honest. The devil sounds so evil, and I don't find myself to be evil at all. Satan just brings chills to my spine," he answers that while air quoting *evil* both times. "Now that the formalities are done, you're just in time."

Bryan stands up from his knees and brushes the dust from the ceiling off his clothes. "Just in time? Just in time for what, and why is your head like that?"

Lucifer laughs even more. "My head? My friend, this is my natural form now. Since I was shunned from heaven and lost my angelic form. God has a funny way of doing things sometimes. I always told him I was fascinated with the cows he made." Lucifer reaches to his desk and picks up a glass. "Now you're just in time to try my new concoction."

"Concoction? What concoction?" asks Bryan while staring at Lucifer's face in amazement and slight disgust.

"You're staring Bryan…that isn't polite. Didn't your mom teach you anything? You act like you've never seen a bull's head before."

"Yes, I have, but never attached to a body like yours. Also speaking English instead of mooing," answers Bryan.

"Ouch. A body like mine? I thought I had a body like Marilyn Monroe," he says as he laughs some more. "Well, now you've seen a head like mine on a body like mine, so stop staring. It's making me uncomfortable…and a tad creeped out."

"Sorry, Satan," Bryan says.

"Oh, please call me Lucifer. Now, are you ready, my friend?" Lucifer replies.

Bryan, looking confused, answers, "Ready for your concoction, Lucifer?"

Lucifer laughs. "Someone get this man a cookie! Yes! So are you ready?"

Bryan, still looking confused, says, "What is this concoction?" As Bryan finished his question, a demon with red skin and tears and cuts all over his body appeared next to him. The demon looks hideous with his face looking like a mix between human and bull with snot running from his nose. The demon is holding an oatmeal raisin cookie. Bryan looks at the demon with disgust. "Uh…I prefer chocolate chip." The demon disappears, then reappears in seconds with a chocolate chip cookie in his nasty-looking hand that only contains three large fingers and one larger thumb. "Gee…thanks," Bryan says as he slowly grabs the cookie out of the demon's hand.

"I'm sorry about that, he's new. We're supposed to offer chocolate chips first. Now! You had a great question before. This concoction is made up of various things, but the main base is demon blood," Lucifer says to Bryan.

"Oh, demon blood? I think I'm allergic to demon blood," Bryan answers hesitantly.

"Don't be silly, Bryan. Nobody has ever been allergic to demon blood. Right?" Lucifer answers as he turns away like he is debating with himself.

The demon answers in a grunt voice that sounds like a munchkin from *The Wizard of Oz*. "Not to my knowledge, sir, but there was that one guy that swelled up and burst after drinking it." Then he disappears.

Lucifer looks at the demon with an eyebrow up. "Hmm. I don't think that had anything to do with the demon blood, I think. Either way, just try it, Bryan. You'll be okay." Then Lucifer reaches behind his back and pulls out a bottle that resembles a beer bottle but red.

Bryan looks around Lucifer and puts a finger in the air. "Where did you get that from?"

"Don't you worry about that, Bryan, I had to keep it warm," Lucifer answers while handing the bottle over.

"No, I must not."

Lucifer grew huge and even more red. "Oh, but I insist!" he yells in a deep, scary voice.

Bryan cowers down a bit and holds out his hand that is now trembling. "Since you insist," he says while grabbing the bottle. Bryan examines it and takes the lid off. He gives it a big sniff that makes his face pucker as if he just tried a lemon. Bryan looks up to Lucifer and gives him eyes, hoping it's just a joke. Lucifer stares with a smile and nods his head yes. Bryan puts the bottle to his lips and takes a small swig. "Wow. It's not too bad," Bryan said then started chugging the bottle.

"Umm…slow down, Bry…it's five hundred and eighty proof," Lucifer says with enthusiasm.

Bryan stops the chug and lowers the bottle. "Five hundred and eighty proof? Like alcohol?"

Lucifer smiles, "Why, yes, my friend. The most potent drink ever made!"

Bryan begins to slur. "The most pote…" He pauses. "Pote… poite…poitant. Umm…" The world begins to sway around Bryan, and everything begins to get hazy. He starts to get blurred vision like he's never had before. "Pointer…five hundred…eight…poof."

"Oh, boy…hey, guys, he blasted," Lucifer says out of the side of his mouth like someone was standing beside him.

Out pops the demon from earlier with the cookie. "I told you he couldn't handle it," the demon says in his grunt, raspy voice.

Then pops in another demon just as ugly. "Yeah, but I said he wouldn't fall. He's still standing, sir." Lucifer shakes his head in disappointment and reaches into his pocket, pulling out a twenty-dollar bill. "Yes, you both were correct," he says as he hands the twenty to the demon that said Bryan would fall.

Bryan, now swaying badly, says, "I…I…I don't freel…fell… good." After Bryan finishes that sentence, he falls forward on his chest and face. Lucifer looks at the demon on his right with the twenty and swipes it from his meaty clutch. Both demons then disappear while Lucifer stares down at Bryan on the floor.

"You better not die on my floor, man," Lucifer says as he nudges Bryan with a hoof. Bryan, however, is going through a whole ordeal of his own. In his head, he's walking through a meadow of roses that smell beautiful. Then he sees a dark cloud rushing in over the meadow. It turns gloomy, and the roses begin to wilt and turn grey. He hears the echo of Lucifer's laughter as the sky turns red. He gets up and tries to run for safety. As he runs, he feels the drink kick back in, and the drunk feeling overwhelms him. He begins to stumble and fall, but he keeps getting back up and trying harder. As he falls again, the ground begins to break off around him and spread apart. It leaves him on his own island. Bryan tries to stand but falls to the edge. His face hovers over the edge, and all he sees is the deep dark well of the abyss. Bryan stands again and makes a leap to the next island of ground floating near him. He reaches the edge and grabs hold of it. Now he's hanging from it.

"Help!" Bryan cries out. "Help!"

Lucifer walks up to him and looks down at Bryan. He says in a deep, evil voice, "I should've led with it's five hundred and eighty proof." Then he puts his hoof to Bryan's forehead and pushes from the edge. Bryan falls while he screams in terror, plummeting down to the abyss.

Chapter 5

BRYAN AWAKENS IN a pool of his own vomit. He still feels dazed and a little drunk. He wipes his mouth clean of any excess vomit with his left arm and begins to stand up. He's wobbly, but he manages to make it to his feet. He looks up and sees that he's back in front of the store where he entered earlier. It's almost as if the store spit him out itself. *I'm back in the mall? Or did I ever actually leave at all?* he questions himself in his head. He tries to gather his composure as he moves in between the crowd of people to a nearby bench to sit down.

He sits down and wipes his eyes trying to figure out if anything is real. If he just met Satan and got smashed on a half of a beer. As he stares off into space, he hears a female voice call to him, "Are you okay? You seem lost."

Bryan answers, "I am." Then he shakes his head and looks up at her. He sees that it's the woman from earlier standing right in front of him. She looks younger now though. About five years younger than before, and now he can see that she has bright blue eyes and blonde hair. She appears to be around eighteen now. "You actually notice me?" he questions.

"Yes, I've noticed you a few times. Each time you look more and more lost," the woman replies. "Why wouldn't I notice you?"

"Why do you look younger than before?" Bryan asks her.

The woman giggles a cute giggle with her hand over her mouth. "Answering a question with a question, that's a classic. I didn't think I was getting younger."

Bryan pauses for a moment and thinks, *Maybe I'm just imagining that she's getting younger.* He then answers, "Never mind that, it's just good that someone notices me. I've been lonely recently. I also got drunk with Lucifer."

She gathers confusion on her face. "With who?"

"Never mind that too," Bryan says while chuckling.

"I don't see why nobody has noticed you. I think that might be all in your head," she replies. "But maybe it's because you're acting like a strange guy." She chuckles. "What's your name?"

"I'm Bryan. What's your name?"

She says her name, but a chime goes off as she says it and prevents Bryan from hearing it. He goes to ask her again, and she pulls him up. "Let's go," she said as she led him up and through the crowd. He watches her long blonde hair as it appears to blow in the wind, but there isn't any wind at all. He wonders where she's taking him as he follows her but has this feeling like he trusts her. There's something about her presence that feels familiar to him, but he just can't place it. Her face looks semifamiliar to him but still not enough for him to know who she is.

She leads him to an elevator, and they step into it, the door closing behind them. "I didn't know these existed anymore. I've just been seeing stairs everywhere," Bryan says.

She pushes the top floor button that reads number twelve. "An elevator? Yeah, they still exist. Crazy, right?" she says with a smile.

Bryan sees the number twelve and looks at it in astonishment. "There are twelve floors in this mall? It must look like a tower from the outside."

She laughs. "This floor is my favorite though. It's out of this world."

Just then the elevator dings and comes to an abrupt stop and the door opens. "Go ahead, Bryan. You go first," she demands while extending her arms toward the door like a guide. He sees nothing but black and hesitates, but then slowly steps out onto the deck. He looks back and the door closes with her still inside.

"Hey! Stop! No, don't close!" he shouts as he taps the open button repeatedly. "I didn't even get your name!" he yells as he brings it to a sigh. He dwells on his feelings for her, knowing that he knows her somehow. *Maybe not your face, but I know your spirit and soul,* he thinks with his head down in sadness. He turns around and sees outer space surrounding him. The whole galaxy was right before his eyes. He sees planets and stars so brightly. "How can this be real? How can I breathe right now?" he questions out loud, knowing he won't get an answer. He looks down and notices he's on a small platform that's only about five feet by five feet with railing all around it.

He looks back around at the breathtaking beauty that is all around him, the stars and planets floating in unison. "It's just so beautiful."

A deep echoing voice answers him from nowhere, "Isn't it?"

Bryan jumps in fear and looks around but sees nobody. "Who's there?"

The voice answers, "I've been waiting for you, Bryan. I've seen your whole life."

"God? Is that you?" Bryan questions.

"You still have much to learn and much to do, Bryan. People depend on you," the voice says back.

"Am I dead?"

"Not yet, Bryan!" the voice yells so loudly that it makes Bryan's ears ring. It softens back up and it says, "But you will soon enough. The choices you make until then all depend on you. They affect not just you but the people around you."

"I know this. I've tried to make good decisions," Bryan says with conviction.

The voice rises and yells, "Have you!" Then it softens back up before saying, "If you have, then you wouldn't be in the mess you're in, Bryan."

Bryan yells back this time, "I didn't know she was seventeen! She told me she was eighteen!"

The voice rises even louder than before, "That's not what I'm talking about, Bryan!" Then it softens back up. "You shouldn't have been out that night. You had work, you had a responsibility. You chose to ignore your responsibilities. For what? For what, Bryan?"

"For fun. I deserve fun, don't I?" Bryan said.

The voice now yells with a fiery tone that shakes the platform. "Fun! For fun, Bryan Butler!" Then the voice softens back up. "You're allowed to have fun, Bryan. Taking advantage of a drunk female is not fun though. Begging for pictures while she is intoxicated isn't fun though. That is taking advantage of someone who can't really decipher her own thoughts."

"I don't know what to say. I regret wha—" Bryan is cut off by the rising fiery voice once again.

"Do you! Do you, Bryan Butler! You regret exactly what?" The voice subsides to its soft tone. "You regret nothing but being caught, don't you, Bryan?"

Bryan speaks back up, "That's not true. I regret it all. I'm filled with regret. I feel bad for letting the people in my life down as well as myself. That bothers me every day, knowing I can't go back and change it all. So don't tell me I don't regret it." Bryan begins to sob uncontrollably. "I can't take it back, but I can change. I'm only human. I've made mistakes, and I don't always think about my actions before I do them. I've learned from all my mistakes. Every damn one of them that I've ever made. It's what makes me a better person moving forward."

"I hope this is true, Bryan Butler. I hope what I've seen isn't the path you truly choose. After all, nothing is written in stone unless you write it yourself. For if you don't change your selfish ways, Bryan Butler, then may I have mercy on your soul." As the voice finishes the sentence, the deck gives out from under Bryan. He starts trying to grab the rail but to no avail. He falls through and looks up, watching the elevator slowly fade out of sight. His screams blast into the nothingness of space.

Chapter 6

HE OPENS HIS eyes as he's screaming, only to find himself back on his mat. He gives it a kiss but then notices that he's still in the mall. "No. No. No," he repeats as he looks around, seeing people walk past him just enjoying their days. The stores are still blurred out, and he's still in his faded blue jeans and white T-shirt.

He gets up and begins to pace back and forth. *This mat must be the key to getting me back to reality. Maybe if I sleep on it, it'll take me back.* He snaps his fingers like he just had a brilliant idea and lays down on the mat, then covers himself up. He closes his eyes and attempts to fall into a sweet sleep. No matter how much he tried, however, he just couldn't. His mind was just racing, and he felt so awake. More awake than he has ever felt in his whole life. He lay there for almost an hour with no sign of getting tired. He just tossed and turned while he huffed and puffed in frustration.

"What the fuck!" Bryan yells as he stands back up. "I'm going crazy. I have gone crazy. This is me in a loony bin. Jesus, please help me!"

"What's up, Bryan? I don't think Jesus will help you," a familiar voice said. "He's more of a figure-it-out-yourself kind of guy. Then God will show you the way. Blah, blah, blah."

"Lucifer!" Bryan yells. "What are you doing here?"

"I go where I want to go to, Bryan," Lucifer answers.

"Can you help me?"

Lucifer laughs. "Help? That depends on what you need and what's in it for me."

Bryan grabs Lucifer's shoulders. "I need out of here. I need you to get me out of here. Am I going crazy?"

Lucifer peers over at Bryan's hands on his shoulders and says, "Crazy? Yes, you're crazy." Then he shrugs off Bryan's hands and dusts off his shoulders. "Don't ever...ever touch me like that again, crazy man. Now, as for your question, I may be able to help you. What's in it for me?"

Bryan hesitates and starts to think. "What do you want?"

Lucifer smiles a huge smile, then leans in close. He says to Bryan in a sinister voice, "Your soul." Then he leans back out and, in his normal voice, says, "What else would I want?"

Bryan steps back and thinks hard. *If he's asking for my soul, then he doesn't have it just yet. This all must be a test. I must do this on my own.* He looks up at Lucifer and says, "Never mind."

"Wait a minute, man. You can't just ask for my help and tease your soul, then just take it back."

Bryan shakes his head. "I just did. I need to figure this out on my own. I need to make a better choice than to ask for your help."

Lucifer touches his chest in shock. "Ouch! That hurts, Bryan. Now you're starting to piss me off. You sound just like that weakling Jesus Christ. I didn't like him very much, Bryan. He turns water into wine, and everyone oohs and aahs. Well, I bet he never made five hundred and eighty proof wine!"

"I need to go, Lucifer. You have a good day," Bryan says with a wave.

Lucifer, feeling insulted, says, "I hope you have a shitty day, Bryan. I hope you don't kill yourself or trust God. Oh, and you're never trying any of my beers ever again!"

Bryan turns toward the crowd of people and walks into them and doesn't look back at Lucifer. He feels good about this move. He knows deep down it was the right choice. One of many he plans on making from now on.

He hears the voices of the little boys again and notices they are still playing catch with the small football. "Over here!" he yells toward the boys. He claps his hands together, and the boy with the football throws it to Bryan. "Atta boy, Joe Montana," he says enthusiastically. He throws it to the second boy who catches it with one hand. "There you go, Jerry Rice. Nice catch!" He claps his hands, and the boy throws it right back. Bryan calls the third boy over, and the boys run to him. "I'll throw you the ball if you tell me what you meant earlier when I asked where we were. You said that I knew. What did that mean?"

The boy slowly begins to back up into the crowd. "I can't tell you that. You must figure it out on your own." Then he disappears along with the other boys.

"Wait! Your ba…" he says, then realizes the football disappeared as well. *I have a lot to figure out*, he thinks.

Bryan paces between the crowd of people walking around, trying to think of where he could possibly be. He paces as if he doesn't see the people any longer; he figures if they don't see him, then why bother paying attention to them.

"You know?" he repeats to himself with a thinking face. "He can't tell me, so I have to figure it out on my own. He said I know, so does that mean I'm in my own subconscious?" he questions himself. "Maybe I am dreaming. Maybe this is reality though? God may be teaching me a lesson? Like a valuable life lesson or an epiphany or something? Maybe the only way out is to figure out my purpose or how to change my life, like God told me I need to do."

Bryan just racks his brain over this whole world he's now entered but can't draw any true conclusions to it at all. Nothing makes sense, but it feels to him like it should. Everything around him for some reason feels safe and normal in a way, but at the same time, it confuses him like a sudoku puzzle. He thinks about the woman and how he can't place her but how she feels comforting to him. How she is the only feeling of actual normality in this whole twilight zone of a subconscious dream he feels he's having. He feels it's not fully a dream as he usually has more control while he's asleep.

"What if this reality and my jail time was a dream the whole time?" he ponders this statement with a strong hope that it's true but, at the same time, maybe not. No jail time seems enticing to Bryan, but this world he's in is too much, too insane, and all over the place for him.

As he stands in the middle of the crowd, thinking out loud, a hand grabs his shoulder. Before he can turn to see who it is, he blasts into another dark portal of his mind. He's starting to know that the pitch black doesn't hurt him but brings him to another world. What world will Bryan land in next? As he feels like he's floating through purgatory, he thinks that this must be another test, another chance to redeem himself. Another opportunity to show his progress and change. He must make good decisions, for if he does, God may release him from this reality.

After many spirals and wind rushing his face, he lands hard. He opens his eyes to see a hospital room. This time, he can't get up, he can't move. He hears voices talking and a doctor at the end of the bed, facing whoever is in the hospital bed. Everyone is a blur but the voices sound familiar. He knows these voices, but he can't tell who they are. The woman is screaming in pain and the doctor is doing something like he's trying to calm her. The blurred figure beside her is doing the same, talking in a calm tone. "Oh! Ow! It's coming!" The woman screams in obvious pain.

Bryan thinks that maybe it's his birth. Now he feels like he's having *A Christmas Carol* effect. He's Ebenezer Scrooge, and all the worlds he's brought to are to show him or test him on how to improve. *What does my birth have to do with all this?* he thinks as he remains stuck on the floor unable to move.

"I see a head!" the doctor screams happily. Bryan watches with intensity as nobody gets to witness their own birth firsthand. The screaming intensifies as the woman feels the coming through. "That's right. Almost done now. One final push." He hears the woman scream loudly then relief as if the body finally dropped out of her at once. Then quiet, just calm quietness, fills the room. A baby begins to cry, and the doctor and nurse swaddle the child in some blankets to clean it off. "Here's your baby girl!" the doctor said with joy.

"Girl?" Bryan whispered to himself. "Oh my...Brenda?" He realizes this was the birth of his daughter. Tears begin to fill his eyes as he weeps. He didn't witness the birth of his daughter, which is something he regrets so much in his life. He sees his daughter wrapped up in blankets as she quits crying because she feels the calm tenderness of her mother. Her face appears to him as he tries to watch through his tears. "Brenda," he says with great sadness. "I miss you so much, baby girl." Pain begins to swell his heart. He feels his chest get tighter as his heart swells more and more. His breathing begins to slow, and his heart grows to the size of a watermelon and then explodes out of his chest.

He's now standing in his living room, holding Brenda with so much joy. "Still got that new baby smell," he says with a smile while looking at Brenda's mother, holding a tear in his eye. "I love her so much."

Kara smiles and giggles at Bryan. "Do you really?"

"Of course, I do. I'll always love little Brenda," he replies with sincerity in his words. "I just hope I'm a good father to her."

Kara frowns and puts her hand on his shoulder. "Of course, you will be. Why wouldn't you be?"

Bryan smiles at Brenda while staring into her beautiful blue eyes. "I don't know, Kara. I just always end up letting everyone down in my life," he says while smiling uncontrollably at Brenda.

"That all comes down to you, Bryan. Brenda is your life now. That means you always must think about her. You can't be selfish with a daughter."

Bryan looks back at Kara. "I'm not selfish. I'm always thinking of others."

"Maybe you try, but you really don't think of others, Bryan. You think about yourself a lot, sometimes too much," Kara says.

"How can you say that?" Bryan asks in insulted anger.

"Where were you when Brenda was born? You should have been there for her birth. You weren't though. You'd think that would be something you didn't want to miss," Kara says back.

Bryan looks back at Brenda and smiles. "I wish I didn't miss it, Kara. I wish I could go back and change that already, but I can't."

"I wish…I wish…I wish…you can wish all you want, but that doesn't change the past. Nothing will change the past, Bryan. Do you wanna know what will help you? Just do. Just be there and do instead of missing out and wishing."

Bryan continues to stare at Brenda with his heart filling with joy. "That's the goal, Kara."

"Don't just say that and continue being selfish. You must want to be."

"I do want to be, Kara. It's not easy changing overnight," says Bryan.

Kara looks at Bryan with disappointment. "It really is easy when you have a good enough reason to change. If you don't, then your daughter must not be a good enough reason."

"Don't ever say that! Don't you ever say that to me! You already question my love for her."

"I'm not the one questioning it, you are, Bryan," Kara responds as her voice echoes away and she fades out of sight. Bryan looks down at Brenda, and she too fades into oblivion, leaving nothing but his empty arms.

Everything around him dulls down to a gloomy gray and appears old and decrepit. Loneliness surrounds his soul, and the feeling of emptiness overwhelms his mind. The echo of Kara's voice engulfs his ear canals. "I'm not the one questioning it, you are, Bryan." It repeats, "You are, Bryan." And once more, "You are."

Bryan's eyes open wide as he says, "I am." Thoughts rush his mind and flood his brain, but one thought sticks out. *I doubted myself. I doubted my ability to raise my daughter. Nobody doubted me but me. I questioned myself and set myself up for failure. I created my failing of Brenda.*

Just then, a rush of wind grabs Bryan and sweeps him up. It swirls him into darkness once again and carries him back to the mall—to the exact same spot before he was carried after the hand grabbed him.

Chapter 7

HE APPEARS IN the middle of the crowd, sucking in a deep breath as if he didn't breathe that whole time and needs air. His eyes open hugely, making it look like he had a breakthrough idea. "My doubt!" he yells with excitement. "My doubt hurts me. I can't doubt it any longer. I have to trust myself and trust my own instincts. My doubt creates selfishness and selfishness creates bad decisions. Is that what I have to learn?" He finished while looking up to God awaiting an answer. "Hello? Am I right?"

Suddenly, an elevator appears before his eyes, and he rushes to it. Now he has the feeling that he's been sent back to reality. Ready to start fresh and change his ways. He jumps into the elevator and presses the button for the twelfth floor. He feels anxious and restless; he feels like the elevator isn't moving fast enough. The elevator goes off with a ding, but it stops on the eighth floor. The door opens, but he begins hitting the twelfth-floor button repeatedly.

"No. No. No. No!" he screams in frustration at the buttons. The door, however, remains open, and the elevator sits still awaiting Bryan's departure. "Are you serious right now?" he questions God. The sound of thunder erupts throughout the elevator, rocking it with ferociousness like an earthquake.

"Okay…fine," he says as he surrenders to the Almighty. He steps out and turns back to the elevator, only to see the doors close and vanish into thin air. "Oh boy…what now," he says as he turns back to see his next lesson.

He sees a courtroom filled with people. All their faces are a blur. The judge sits at his desk in the front of the room, high up on a pedestal. His face too is a blur. The sound of people talking and chanting fills the courtroom. The judge bangs his gavel three times and yells, "Order! Order!" The whole courtroom silence instantly. "We are gathered here today to judge a selfish poor soul. A man so despicable and disgusting, that it's hard to even call him a man at all. The state versus Bryan Butler. Let's get started with the trial of Bryan Butler."

Bryan uncontrollably moves to the center of the room like he's being pushed by ghosts he can't see. Bryan looks around the room with fear and heavy anxiety, bringing sweat to his face. He can't control any of this, and the fear of not knowing what's next sets in.

"Bryan Butler! You are here today for your crimes against society. Crimes against your peers, your family, and against yourself. How do you plea?" the judge asked.

Bryan takes a big gulp and answers, "Not guilty, your honor." Instantly the gallery begins talking and whispering among themselves.

The sound of the gavel echoes through the room. "Order! Order!" the judge howls. The gallery is instantly in silence once again. "Not guilty, you say? What makes you not guilty? We're all guilty of something, so what makes you not guilty?"

"Umm…your honor, I may have made mistakes, but we all have. Everyone deserves a second chance," Bryan says with determination.

The judge leans forward in his chair. "A second chance? How many chances do you believe you deserve? I've seen your life, and quite frankly, your whole life has been a second chance. A third, fourth, fifth, sixth, and more!"

Bryan gulps again. "Your honor, I've never had a second cha—" Then the judge interrupts him.

"You've never had a second chance? How selfish of you to ignore all your chances in life. You've had chances galore but squandered every damn one of them. You grab hold of every chance you've received and selfishly stomped it into the ground."

Bryan steps back from the altar where the judge presides. "Maybe you're right. I know the error of my ways now, your honor. I know what I must do."

"Do you? Do you, Bryan Butler?" the judge squawks with seriousness.

"Yes, your honor. I know that I need to be less selfish. I need to think of others before myself when it matters. I also need to stop doubting my abilities because all that leads to bad decisions," Bryan says with conviction.

The judge as well as the gallery begin to laugh in unison. "You still don't fully get it! You're blind to what's around you. You're blind to him, Bryan Butler. You still have much more to learn. For that, I find you guilty! You're sentenced to death! Send him to floor nine, bailiff!"

The bailiff grabs ahold of Bryan and drags him across the floor. He drags up to the elevator, now behind the judge's pedestal, and tosses him in with force. Bryan hits the elevator floor hard, and the bailiff reaches in pressing the ninth floor and quickly steps out. The elevator door closes and starts moving up.

The elevator door opens, and Bryan slowly gets to his feet. He looks out of the door and around to see what his surroundings look like now. He sees nothing so far but then steps out, and the door closes behind him. It's just dark, and Bryan is left in his own self-pity. "I don't know what you want from me!" he yells into the darkness. After those words leave his mouth, the dark begins to swirl around.

Now Bryan is left in his cell back at the jail. The drip of the leaky faucet echoes in the small cell. The feel of the cold concrete chills him to the bone. The spine-tingling noise of the metal doors shutting rumbles throughout. He shivers from the sound of the doors and the feel of cold air brushing his neck.

"Well, I hope you're happy," a voice echoes into his cell. The image of Kara is now forming in front of his cell door. "Are you even listening to me?"

Bryan runs to the door and grabs hold of the cold bars. "Yes! I'm listening to you, Kara. I'm not happy at all. I just want to hold Brenda again."

"You'll never get that chance again. I'd say I'm sorry, but it's not my fault," Kara responds with sadness in her eyes, a tear almost forming in her left eye.

Bryan reaches out his hand, but Kara backs away. "No, it's my fault. I can't take back my actions. I can't change the outcome, it's too late."

"Is it, Bryan? Is it too late? In my opinion, it's never too late until you're buried six feet in the ground. There's always time and chances as long as your heart desires it," Kara says with more tears falling from both eyes.

"But I'm sentenced to death," says Bryan with guilt in his eyes.

"You're not dead yet," Kara responds with a slight smile forming. "You have a road from here to death. Along that road, you'll see more obstacles. Every chance you get adds up, and he sees it. He sees them all. He knows when you're leading with him at the helm and when you're just leading yourself. All he wants is for you to trust. Trust yourself, trust your life, and most importantly, trust in him."

"I don't know how to, Kara. I don't know how to trust in anything," Bryan states.

Kara grabs his hand that's still extended out to her. "Well, I guess that's what you have to figure out on your own. Maybe trust your daughter some time." Kara lets go of Bryan's hand and steps back. "Sometimes you have to learn to let go before you choose to hold on." Kara backs up until she vanishes into the wall.

Guards file in as soon as she disappears. "Butler! Let's go! It's chow time," one guard blurts as the cell door opens. They grab his arms and drag him out of his cell. His feet scrape the concrete floor as they carry him out into the cafeteria. They toss him into the crowd of inmates and then disappear.

Bryan picks himself up to his feet and grabs a tray. He begins moving with the line. "Chicken or beef?" the lunch lady solicits.

"Um…chicken?" he proclaims with doubt. She laughs and scoops brown muck up and slaps it on his tray. He glances down and sees worms and maggots infesting the slop. He gives a disgusted look and keeps moving down the line. Another lunch lady tosses a molding corn bread onto his tray. He finally reaches the end of the line and takes his tray from the bar. He then walks to a table and sits down.

"You're in my seat," a little person proclaims from behind Bryan.

Bryan turns and sees who is talking to him. "I'm here first, little man."

The little person grows bigger to about seven feet tall. "Still being selfish, I see," he remarks with great fiery. Then he grabs Bryan and picks him up with one hand. "Not so generous and considerate, are you?"

"I'm sorry." Bryan gives in while dangling from the man's grasp.

The man then announces, "Not yet, you aren't."

A tray hits Bryan in the back as hard as a car hitting a wall. Bryan falls from the clutches of the man and lands on the floor, almost breathless. All the inmates begin to stand and surround Bryan who's trying to catch his breath. As he looks up to them all around him, they begin to kick him unmercifully. Bryan grabs his head and curls into the fetal position. They continue to kick and stomp Bryan in anger and hate. Blood begins to splatter out from the crowd's feet.

"Help! Help me! Guards, help!" Bryan cries but to no avail. Bryan closes his eyes and feels the suffocation of death succumb to him and grip his soul. He squeezes his eyes together as hard as he can and in moments doesn't feel a thing. He opens his eyes only to see he's back in the mall, on the floor, with a crowd of people walking past him.

Bryan sits up and sighs at the people just stepping past him. *What more do I have to go through?* he thinks. *What more do I have to learn?* He knows deep down he has more to learn and know. He has more wisdom to unearth in his mind. He just hopes he can piece it together into one big life lesson. He knows that God must be trying to tell him something, but the answers haven't been totally clear to Bryan. He brings himself to his feet and walks over to the water fountain in the middle of the food court.

Chapter 8

THE FOUNTAIN IS so majestic. It's carved out of rock, with an angel as its centerpiece. There is a horn the angel is holding up to its mouth and water flows from the horn. It's a huge centerpiece inside of a huge fountain that has a bench made of stone going all around it. Bryan sits down on the bench and actually feels the splash of the water trickle to his forehead. He reaches up and wipes the water with the back of his hand, feeling the cool wetness that it leaves behind. He leans forward and puts his hand into the cool water, moving it back and forth in a sway motion. It messes up his reflection, but he doesn't want to see himself at the moment. He just enjoys the feel of the water between his fingers. It makes him feel calm, the calmest he's been since the woman talked to him.

"Hello, there," a calm quiet voice said from beside him. "It's my birthday in fourteen days. March 16. My name is John, what's yours?"

Bryan sees a hand extended in front of his face and follows it with his eyes to a short older gentleman sitting next to him. This man was completely bald with a full beard that was white as snow. His skin was brown, and he was chubby. His face brought a feeling of joy like Santa's face in commercial ads. His nose was long and big. His eyes were beady and brown. "My name is Bryan, nice to meet someone who actually sees me," Bryan states as he reaches his hand out to shake John's.

"Nobody else sees you?" John inquires.

"Not many, John. Just you and a girl, oh, and um…another guy, but you'll think I'm crazy if I told you who," Bryan remarks with a chuckle.

"Well, Bryan, it's nice to meet you too! Sometimes in life, we're ignored. Sometimes in life, we're not ignored. The ones that matter tend to see us though."

Bryan shrugs. "I guess you're right."

John laughs slightly and smiles sincerely. "The ones that ignore us don't matter. Yet not all the ones that don't ignore us do matter."

"That makes sense, John. Do you write fortune cookies?" Bryan queries.

John continues to smile at Bryan with the sincerest smile he's ever noticed. "I've written a lot of stuff before, a long time ago. Never forget, though, we choose in our lives who should matter and who doesn't. So you should always choose wisely."

"I'll keep that in mind," Bryan says back. He looks down and sees a box sitting on John's lap. "What do you have there?"

John looks down at the box. "Why, it's a box of chocolates."

Bryan laughs. "Like *Forrest Gump*?"

John chuckles with him. "Yes, you could say that, Bryan. There are exactly three hundred and thirty-six pieces of chocolate in this box."

"Wow!" Bryan exclaimed with astonishment. "Did you count them all?"

John shakes his head with another chuckle. "No, my friend. The man that gave me this box told me how many were in here, and I trust his word."

"That's hard for me to do, John. I couldn't trust that. I mean, the box is awfully small. Don't you think?"

John looks down at the box, then back up to Bryan. "That may be, but the man that gave me this box hasn't let me down yet."

Bryan replies, "Have you looked in the box yet? Maybe there isn't even chocolate at all."

John continues to smile that sincere smile he has. There's no need to look. If I can't trust his word, then I have no faith in him. A world without faith is a world of destruction."

Bryan stares into John's kind eyes, practically speechless, and finally musters up a response. "You've got a lot of wisdom, John. Who are the chocolates for?"

John chuckles some more. "For someone special. Someone in need of them."

Bryan laughs hysterically. "Who needs three hundred and thirty-six pieces of chocolate?"

John just continues to smile for a moment avoiding Bryan's response. "I've been here for three hundred and fifteen days. Waiting for that person to show up."

"That seems like an awfully long time. Are the chocolates still good?"

John replies, "They are."

Bryan, with a sincere look, says to John, "I hate to tell you, John, but I don't think they're showing up."

John stands up and extends his hand to Bryan. "Oh, I have faith that they'll receive this box." Bryan grabs his hand and shakes it. "I'll see you around, Bryan. Have a good day." Then John lets go of Bryan's hand and walks off.

Bryan looks down at where John is sitting and notices he left the box of chocolates on the bench. "Hey, John!" he hollers and looks up toward John walking away. "You forgot yo—" Bryan pauses as he doesn't see John any longer. Bryan picks up the box and holds it on his lap. "Must not have been that important."

Chapter 9

TEMPTATION OVERWHELMS HIM. He stares down at the box while he fights the urge to open it up. His mind tells him to do it, but his consciousness says that he can't. Still, he wants to see if there are truly three hundred and thirty-six pieces of chocolate inside. He finds himself slowly lifting the lid. He reaches a finger in, edging closer and closer to the sweet treats. He looks around to see if John is coming back for them but sees nobody that cares. As he touches a piece, he hears the familiar chime go off. He feels that familiar presence gathering around his soul. He feels comforted once again. The chime goes off a second time, but as he looks, he can't see where it's coming from. He sat the box down on the bench beside him and stood to look around more.

He begins to hear the chewing and mushing of food beside him. "Dang, Bryan, your chocolate is delicious!" she says with excitement.

"Hey! Those are fo…" he says, then pauses as he notices it is the woman—only she isn't a woman no longer. She's a teenager, maybe fifteen years of age. "Hi, there. Sorry about that. Thought you were someone else," he says as he grabs the box from her. "You mustn't eat those. They're a gift for someone."

"Who?" she inquires.

"I don't know exactly," he answers.

"You don't know? But you know they're a gift?" the girl questions.

"It's hard to explain. Some guy left them here. He said he was waiting to give them to someone."

She ponders what he told her for a moment. "Well, maybe that someone arrived."

Bryan laughs. "Well, if they did, then we wouldn't have the box now, would we?"

"No, I guess we wouldn't," she says then stops to think a moment longer. "Unless…the box was left for the intended person, and the intended person is now in possession of them."

Bryan glares at her with satisfaction. "You know, you're a smart girl for your age. What are you like twelve?"

"Umm…I'm fifteen, thank you very much," she says back with sass.

"My bad." Bryan laughs. "So you're fifteen now? You're saying this box may be intended for me? I didn't even know the guy. He said his name was John."

"You may not have known who he was but maybe he knew who you were."

Bryan pauses and thinks hard about what she has said. "How can someone be waiting for me that I don't even know?"

She grabs the box from Bryan and opens it back up. "He works in mysterious ways, Bryan. I do believe that this box found its intended person." She reaches in and picks out a chocolate and puts it in her mouth.

"Does it look like there are three hundred and thirty-six pieces in there?" Bryan asks.

Chewing and smacking her lips together with joy, she replies, "I don't know, but this one is orange cream and it's amazing!"

He can hardly understand what she said but asks, "Are there any dark chocolate? Those are my favorite."

She stops and looks up at him with her mouth open and chocolate on her lips. "No way! Dark chocolate is my favorite too!" Excitement fills her face. "You're in luck because I think they're all a form of dark chocolate. Dark chocolate orange cream. Dark chocolate caramel. Dark chocolate turtles!"

"Well, hand me one please," he demands politely.

"Which one would you like?"

"Surprise me," he says back. She reaches into the box and pulls one out from the middle and hands it to him. He grabs it and pops it into his mouth like he just tossed a cashew in from his palm. "Oh my!" he exclaims with total ecstasy.

She sits up from a slouch. "Is it good? Did I give you a bad one?"

He continues to chew and chew. "No, not bad at all. It's so dang good! Or shall I say delectable? The best piece of chocolate I've ever had."

"Really? You think so?" she perks up and questions.

"Yes, I do. It's also my favorite kind of dark chocolate. Dark chocolate crunch! I love the little crispies inside," he replies.

"Wow! That's my favorite one too! Dark chocolate crunch is the best!" she announces with pure excitement.

Bryan looks shocked at this point. "We have a love for chocolate in common. That's for sure. I have to ask you though…when I first saw you, I couldn't see your face at all. Now I can see your eyes and lips. It also seems like every time I see you, you get younger and younger. The younger you get, the more of your face I can see. Why is that?"

She stares blankly at him as he stares back at her. "I don't know what you're talking about, Bryan. My age hasn't changed to my knowledge. My face is my face. If you can't see it, then maybe you're not ready to see it yet."

"Maybe you're right," he says with dissatisfaction. "I still have no clue what's exactly going on, but you seem to know more than I do."

"I think it's all in your head, to be honest with you." Bryan watches her as she finishes her sentence and studies what he sees. He watches her face as she gorges on more chocolate. He sees her blue eyes and her lips. He also sees her nose now and parts of her chin. He can see a little of her cheeks, but they fade in and out. He still can't see who she fully is, but he knows deep down that she is important to him. He can feel it in the pit of his stomach. "Do you want some more chocolate?" she asks, holding a piece in her fingers.

"No, dear. Not right now, but you better slow down before you get a tummy ache."

She smiles a big chocolate smile at him. "I think I'll be fine." Then she put the one in her fingers into her mouth. "I've only eaten like fifty of them."

He smiles big at her and looks down at the box. He notices it really seems like a never-ending box of chocolate. "You know what, I'll take one more. Give me a dark chocolate cluster."

She hands him a cluster, and she takes one as well. They both toss them in their mouth simultaneously and enjoy them together.

As they sit by the fountain enjoying the dark chocolate together, his feeling for her grows even deeper. He feels love for her, but not just any love. He feels unbreakable and unconditional love that can never stop. It overwhelms him to the point of undoubting joy. She looks up at him with her beautiful blue eyes and grabs his hand.

"Do you trust me?" she interrogates.

"Of course, I do," he replies with conviction.

She stands up and he stands with her. She places the box of chocolates on the bench and leads him through the crowd of people. "See this place right here." She points at a storefront. "Go in there."

"Are you coming too?" he asks.

She shakes her head. "No, I'm not. Just like the twelfth floor, you have to do this on your own."

"How do you know this?" he questions. "That I have to go in alone."

"I just do. It comes to me, and I'm guided to guide you. All I know is I can't go in with you."

Bryan hesitates before asking, "Are you going to be here when I come out?"

She smiles. "I'll be around. Now go." Then she pushes him past the threshold.

The darkness of the store closes in on him and sucks him into another whirl of motion. Just like the other times, he spins throughout the darkness. He becomes disoriented from all the rotation, warping Bryan to another world and bringing him to yet another adventure. He pops out and lands with his face in the sand. He looks up and spits sand out of his mouth.

"A desert?" he questions, dumbfounded.

"Actually, the pyramids of Egypt," a snide-sounding voice said from behind him. The man is tall and very lean. He has dark skin and big full lips with a big wide nose to match. His face is considered handsome. His hair is dark black and fluffy like a poodle. His eyes are just as dark as his hair. "But I guess you're right. It is a desert." The voice sounds sophisticated and rich, almost kind of feminine and stuck up. "Are you going to stand, dear boy?"

"Yes," Bryan says while bringing himself to his feet and brushing sand off his clothes.

"Ahh. It's just beautiful, isn't it?" the man says.

Bryan finishes wiping sand off of himself. "Yes, you could say that."

The man looks Bryan up and down. "Wasn't always beautiful like this. It used to be a breeding ground for slaves. Jews that were made to work. Work for practically nothing at all. Then Moses came along and helped free them."

"Yeah, I think I've heard the story before," Bryan replies.

"Yes, of course. Could you imagine carrying all those huge men-cut rocks up that entire thing? In this hot desert heat. All for a king that didn't care about any of them."

"Honestly, I couldn't. Must've been torture," Bryan remarks.

The man huffs. "Torture. Don't get me started on that. They would use children and men to do this. All the old people they deemed worthless were condemned to death. It was a sad time indeed. The Jews, however, suffered many sad times throughout history. Punishment perhaps. They did after all condemn Jesus Christ to death. All in exchange for a man undeserving to be released. Then again, it was for the greater good. If it didn't happen, then our sins wouldn't be forgiven. Call it the final covenant."

"You seem to know a lot about this. Who are you?" Bryan asks.

"Right. Hello, officially. My name is Mark. You must be Bryan Butler." Mark extends his hand for a shake.

Bryan grabs it and reciprocates with a nice firm handshake. "Pleasure to meet you, Mark."

"Yes, I'm sure. A pleasure indeed," replies Mark with his nose turned to the air.

Bryan looks him up and down and notices his clothes. Mark is in what appears to be an adventure outfit. Something like an archeologist topped with a safari hat.

"It's nice to finally talk to someone," Mark exclaims. "I've been waiting here for nine hundred and twenty-four days…or was it nine hundred and twenty-five? I don't know. I've lost count."

"That's a long time. Are you waiting for me?" Bryan asks.

Mark snickers. "Conceited, are you? I've been waiting for my good friend, Luke, but he appears to be late."

"I'm sorry, I just assumed. Is your friend always this late?"

"I'm afraid Luke never pays attention to time. He just shows up when he's needed. Last time, I waited for twelve hundred and thirty days."

Bryan's eyes got big. "You do this a lot then? Waiting must get boring."

"Yes, well, I've got nothing but time. My job nowadays consists of waiting and helping," Mark answers.

"Sorry, I'm late, Mark. To me though, I feel like I'm right on time. It's precisely 9:24 a.m., and that's when he told me to arrive," Luke says out of nowhere. He has an equally sophisticated voice, rich sounding but not as feminine as Mark.

"Oh, Luke. I'm not surprised at all. This here is, Bryan," Mark says while extending a hand toward Bryan. Luke is tall as well. Just as dark but has a bushy dark beard to match his head. His eyes are brown and his nose, flat and wide. His lips are full, but not as thick as Mark's. He too wears an outfit that resembles Mark, topped with a matching hat.

Luke looks Bryan up and down. "You dress awfully funny."

Bryan laughs. "I was going to say the same about you two in your old-style archeologist outfit."

Luke continues looking Bryan up and down with an eyebrow extended upward. "Well, nice insult. You, however, are the one that sticks out like a sore thumb."

Mark snickers some more. "Yes, indeed. An overly huge sore thumb."

Bryan looks down at his outfit and then back to theirs. "Touché."

Luke continues, "Now since we've finished the pleasantries, let's be off." He begins to walk while Mark follows behind. Luke stops and looks back at Bryan who is still standing there. "Come on, old chap. We don't have all day." Bryan shrugs his shoulders and begins following both. "It's exactly six hundred and thirty-seven steps to this pyramid from where we are. That may seem like a lot, but really, it isn't."

Bryan continues to follow them while asking, "You guys are really into precise numbers, aren't you?" Mark squints his eyes a bit and peers back at Bryan. Bryan continues, "The last guy I talked to was into numbers as well. I believe John was his name."

Luke then smiled a big cheesy smile. "John, yes. You remember John, don't you, Mark?"

Mark snickers. "Ah, yes. John is a good man. Very wise."

"Very wise indeed," Luke replies almost in unison. "I think I was forty-eight when I met John. But I'm not entirely sure anymore. It's been a very, very long time."

Bryan gazes at both back and forth with sudden confusion overwhelming his face. "How do you both know him exactly? You don't seem to be the type of man that would know this old man."

Mark bounces with wonder as he pauses to gander at Bryan. "Old man? My dear boy, we are much older than he. What does that make you think of us?"

Bryan is a little nervous. Luke turns as well and says, "You're awful judgy aren't you, dear boy? Looks may be deceiving, so never judge a book by its cover. Judgment is for him." Luke pointed to the sky. "Now, to answer your question though, you could say we're in the same profession."

"Archeology?" Bryan queries.

Mark and Luke glance at each other and begin to chuckle. "You could say that I guess," Mark replies.

"Yes, archeology," Luke says after, and then they both chuckle some more.

Bryan watches as they find great amusement in what he says. Now he figures he may be wrong about the profession these guys are in. "I feel like I'm missing something here."

Luke gives a half smile. "Boy, you're missing a lot right now. This is why we were sent to guide you. If I told you everything, then we'd be doing your job for you."

Mark glances at Luke then back to Bryan. "He's precisely right. There are strict rules for helping lost souls figure out the path. I almost feel like we're saying too much as we speak." They both turn and continue to walk toward the pyramid.

Bryan peers at both of them back in forth with his mouth hanging open, as if he's ready to catch flies. Then he slowly paces behind them in deep thought. *They've said too much? Strict rules? So I am in some sort of dream world. God must be pulling the strings. They mentioned a path. Could they be doing God's work? Am I a project? This whole time John, Luke, and Mark have been waiting specifically for me. It makes sense now. They all seem to reference an unknown leader. John mentioned he trusted "his" word. The word of God? Who are these people though? How were they chosen to help me? Why am I so special to have people to help me like this? What does God see in me to put this time and effort into?* So many questions on Bryan's mind, yet no answers jump out at him. He has been more of a tell-me kind of guy. Never could get subtle hints, and when he did, he ignored them, thinking they weren't hints at all. He would think he misinterpreted what people would say to him. He looked at Mark and Luke as they approached closer to the pyramid. "My job?"

Luke sighs. "You're not very good at this, are you? It's up to you to figure out everything. We are merely pillars of your knowledge and success. Or shall I say…pyramids in your quest." He snickers softly.

"My quest?" Bryan questions.

"Ah, you ask too many questions. Instead of asking questions, you should trust that it's all figured out. You should believe that you're in good hands. Trust in him. Talk to him when you have concerns. He doesn't always answer with words but with signs as well. Be more observant, dear boy!" Mark states with slight urgency.

They reach the bottom of the pyramid. Bryan glances upward to the top, amazed by the height. He is astonished by the sheer size of it. He's seen many pictures of pyramids but has never been this close. Pictures don't do it justice. He finds it hard to believe that there are many, many more pyramids like this around Egypt and other places like Sudan. He feels like ten football fields could be inside of this thing and still have room for thousands of people to watch all the way to the top. The tan look that it gives off with the sun shining so brightly—Bryan always thought they were golden brown or yellow.

"It is breathtaking," Bryan says in awe.

"Yes, breathtaking indeed. One of man's greatest buildings. So many man-hours went into it. So many skilled people didn't make it their profession but perfected it because they had to, or they'd be punished," Luke says.

Mark continues, "Yes, indeed. It's one of those things that is amazing and sad at the same time. Bittersweet as you would say."

They all simultaneously peer up and down the great big pyramid for moments. Luke then looks down at Bryan. "Can you believe we have one hundred and seventy-four more things to do today? We must be shuttling off now."

"How do I get back to where I came?" Bryan asks.

"Oh, I don't think you'll have to worry about that, dear boy. Good day and good luck on your quest to find what you're being shown," Mark says with a sincere smile.

"Yes, good day and Godspeed, Bryan," Luke says as well, then gives a wave.

As Luke finishes his wave to Bryan, a burst of wind picks up and swirls around them. Sand floods their eyesight and forms a vortex around Bryan. "Wait!" Bryan shouts but to no avail. The whirlwind of sand picks him up and carries him up to the sky.

Chapter 10

BRYAN AWAKENS BACK at the mall with sand in his shoes and in his hair. He sat up and brushed his hair out with his hands and then began shaking his head vigorously. He took off both shoes and poured out a lot of sand. Bryan thinks he can build a castle with all the sand that came out. Far more than he ever expected to be in his shoes. He brushes off his socks and puts his shoes back on.

"The numbers?" he questions himself, while now pacing back and forth between the crowds of people. Now he doesn't even notice the people as much. He treats them as if they're ghosts just wandering around and not like obstacles as he did before. "I wish I had a pad and pencil," he mutters as he paces. He pauses and looks down at his left front pocket with amazement. He reaches into his pocket and pulls out a pad and pencil. "Thank you, God," he says while he peered up in disbelief. "What were all those numbers? Ugh, I can't remember. Okay, think, Bryan. Luke said forty-eight." He jots it down. "Six hundred and thirty-seven and definitely one hundred and seventy-four." He writes those numbers down too. "Oh! He also said nine hundred and twenty-four!" He hastily writes it down in excitement. *I'm not sure how I'm remembering these, but I guess I may have some help right now*, he thinks as he now includes God into the mix.

"Okay now. Mark mentioned twelve hundred and thirty." He scribbles it down. "Nine hundred and twenty-four sounds familiar, and he did mention nine hundred and twenty-five. He wasn't sure though." Bryan pencils in both numbers to be safe. *This is a lot easier than I thought it would be. With the help of God, I guess things become easier*, he ponders.

"Okay, now, John. Johnny boy. What numbers did he throw at me? Three hundred and thirty-six for sure!" He prints it on the little pad. "That was the number of chocolates in the box, I won't forget that." He giggles. He ponders more while tapping the pencil on his chin in deep-thinking mode. "He said his birthday was in fourteen days. Maybe his birthday as well!" He writes down fourteen and then three sixteen for his birthday. "Then he told me he was waiting for three hundred and fifteen days." He pencils that number in as well.

After he finishes with all the numbers, he stares blankly at the pad. *What do all these numbers mean though? What purpose do they have? They all mean nothing to me. There has to be something deeper here that I'm missing.*

Bryan walks back to the fountain and sits down on the concrete bench. He leers at the centerpiece angel in thought and concentration. After moments pass, he looks down beside him where that girl is sitting and notices the chocolates are still there. *I'm surprised these weren't stolen. Then again, I don't think any of these people even know where they are either*, he thinks as he opens the box up and pulls out a dark chocolate strawberry cream. He gazes upon it and then slides it into his mouth with such delight. "Still the best chocolate ever," he mumbles with a mouthful of chocolate smashing on his teeth. He grabs one more out, this time a dark chocolate coconut, and eats that one as well.

He hears boys screaming and jumps up, almost knocking the box off of the bench. He looks around with haste, vigorously back and forth past the people. He spots them just ahead still playing catch in between all the people. He sprints over toward them and intercepts the ball right before it reaches the oldest boy. "Ha! Just like Dion!" he says, excited at his reaction time. He tosses the ball over to the middle child, who catches it and gives a stiff arm to nobody at all. It looked like a Heisman pose to Bryan. They toss the ball back and forth for a while, just playing catch and having fun. It makes Bryan feel like a kid again. Just playing around with his father and brother in the backyard. Running routes and using bushes as defenders to catch the ball over. Bryan catches the ball and pauses before asking, "Do you boys want some chocolate?"

The boys start screaming in excitement almost in unison. "Yes, me, me, me!" He takes them over to the bench and shows them the magnificent box full of the delightful treat.

"All right, boys, you each get three pieces since this is the third time I have seen you." He reaches in and pulls out three pieces. One for each of them to start. "First, I want to know your names," he points at the oldest boy.

"My name is Isaiah," the oldest answers, and Bryan hands him one piece.

Then he points to the middle child. "My name is Jeremiah!" the boy says, exhilarated. Bryan hands him one piece too.

Then he points at the smallest of the boys. "My name is Malachi." Bryan hands him the final piece in his hand.

"It's very nice to officially meet you Isaiah, Jeremiah, and Malachi. My name is Bryan," he says with a smile that could've lit up the whole building. "Now each of you reach in and pick out any two chocolates you want."

The boys cheer, and each takes turns reaching into the box, picking out what they think looks best. "Thank you!" the boys scream in unanimity.

"Now, I better not see you boys again, or I'll have to give you each four pieces of chocolate." He giggles. "Have a blessed day."

The boys start to laugh and then yell, "Bye!" and wave as if they were one. Bryan pulled out his pad and pencil and wrote down the names Isaiah, Jeremiah, and Malachi. He stared down at the pad. *I still don't know what all this means, but better be safe than sorry.* He thought while concentrating on all the numbers and names.

The chime sounds off once again and echoes throughout the mall. Bryan looks up from the pad with a passionate smile and looks for the girl of mystery. *She's around here somewhere.* He glances to his right and then to his left. As he looks straight forward, he hears the sound of mushing beside him. "You still have chocolate I see," she says with a mouthful.

He quickly peers down at her and notices she aged down more. She now looks like she is about ten years old. "Yes, dear. Go ahead and help yourself," he says while smiling and showing off his pearly whites, which weren't as white as they could be since Bryan used to smoke cigarettes when he was younger.

"Thank you!" she replies with glee. "Who were those boys?"

"Isaiah, Jeremiah, and Malachi were their names."

She laughs with chocolate in her mouth, smashing into her teeth and tongue. "Just like the Bible!"

He stops smiling and gives a face of wonder. "What do you mean?"

She puts another chocolate into her mouth and chews it up quickly. "They're in the Bible. More importantly, all three are stories in the Bible. Isaiah, Jeremiah, and Malachi I believe are a part of the Israel Prophets stories."

Bryan, now stunned at what he just heard, starts to rattle his brain. *Israel prophets? So this all may be connected to the Bible.* "What about John, Luke, and Mark?"

She giggles, and the sweet little giggle warms his heart. "Those are stories about Jesus in the New Testament. They are saints. Saint John, Saint Luke, and Saint Mark."

"You know a lot about the Bible?" he quizzes her.

"Well, my dad helped with that a lot. He got me into the Bible when I was young. He would read me stories from it at bedtime. They always fascinated me. We would also go to church almost every Sunday, and the pastor taught me some as well," she replies.

"Name off more saints for me please," he demands.

"Um…I think there's only one more from the Bible. Saint Mathew is his name. He is the first in the New Testament for the stories of Jesus." She picks out another chocolate and tosses it into her mouth with satisfaction. "My favorite was always Saint Luke. His stories were the most insightful to me. I also really love James!" Then she picks another chocolate out and eats that one too.

"Who's James?" he asks with an eyebrow in the air. Then he walks his fingers to the box and pulls one out while making direct eye contact with the girl.

"James was a servant of God and the Lord Jesus Christ. He has a lot of wisdom and very good scripture. His story will help with patience." Then she continues to chew the rest of the melted chocolate that is sitting in her mouth.

Bryan slides the chocolate in his hands right between his teeth and begins chewing it. He pulls out his pad and pencil and writes down Mathew and James under John, Luke, and Mark's names. He puts the pad down to her level and shows her the names and numbers. "Do any of these numbers mean anything to you?"

She studied the pad for a few moments then jumped with joy. "Yes! Well…some do. I'm not like…I don't have it all memorized or anything." She points to John 3:16. "For God so loved the world, that he gave his only son, that whoever believes in him should not perish but have eternal life." She smiles and looks at Bryan's face. "That one I thought everyone knew."

Bryan writes down what she said on a separate paper in the pad as she was saying it. "Are there anymore that pop out at you?"

She looks some more and points at John 3:16. "I think this one is whoever believes in the s—"

Bryan stops her. "Hold on, sweetheart. I got to write this down so slow down a bit."

She pauses and gives him a second. "Ready now?" He nods his head yes. "Whoever believes in the Son has eternal life; whoever does not obey the Son shall not see life, but the wrath of God remains on him."

Bryan finishes writing the passage. "Good. Thank you, dear. Now go on, but slowly so I can keep up."

She glances around at the page again. "Okay, Luke! Luke 48 says, 'As Jesus answered, it is written, man shall not live by bread alone, but by every word of God.'" She gazes upon Bryan once more and studies his face as he concentrates on finishing the passage. When he finished, she points at Luke 9:24. "For whoever would save his life shall lose it, but whoever loses his life for my sake will save it."

Bryan writes quickly as she speaks each word to him. "Very good! This kind of starts to make sense to me."

"Luke 1:74 says, 'And if he sins against you seven times in a day, and turns to you seven times, saying, I repent, you must forgive.'"

Bryan finishes writing that one down as well and glances into her blue eyes. The type of blue that looks ice cold but draws you in and mesmerizes you. "You're the smartest little girl I've ever known."

She giggles that sweet soft giggle. "Thank you, but my dad was smart. I learned so much from him." She looks back down at the page and points down at Mark 9:25. "Scratch that one off. I don't believe it fits with the scheme of the rest. 9:24 does, however. 'Immediately, the father of the child cried out and said, "I believe; help my unbelief."'"

Bryan writes it as quickly as she says it. "I'm getting good at writing this down. I find that interesting though, when he told me those numbers he could remember if it was 9:24 or 25. Apparently, 9:24 was the right one." He looks upon the writing. "I do see a common theme indeed."

"Yeah," she answers while picking out another chocolate. "It seems the common theme would be to believe in God and Lord Jesus Christ, and you'll be saved." She throws the chocolate into her mouth and chews with joy. "Mm. Dark chocolate cashew! I love cashews."

"I do too! We really do have food in common. Cashew is my favorite nut."

"Actually, cashew isn't a nut," she responds with a laugh.

"What are they then?"

"They are classified as a drupe."

He raises an eyebrow. "What's a drupe?"

"A drupe is a fleshy fruit with a shell and seed inside of it."

Bryan, shocked, says, "Cashews are fruits?"

"The more you know," the girl responds with a keen look on her face.

"Do me a favor and find me a Bible. We have more numbers to figure out."

She jumps up from the bench and puts her hand on her forehead like an army soldier saluting the flag. "Yes, sir!" she shouts. Then she points down to one of the stores across from the food court. "I'm being told you need to go in there."

"To that store?" He points.

"Yes! That's where he told me you need to visit next."

"Thank you for your help, sweetheart. Now go find me a Bible and meet me here later," he says, smiling uncontrollably. Then he begins rushing over to the store. It's the first time he's going to enter without fear and having willingness in his heart.

She waves at him as he runs off, smiling back with her perfect little smile showing true pearly whites. She grabs another chocolate from the box and begins to skip off in the opposite direction.

Chapter 11

HE STOPS AND stares at the storefront with a resolution in his eyes. He feels better than he has in a long time, finally having a grasp on what is happening to him. He now knows God is teaching him something. Perhaps teaching him how to forgive himself and believe in God, knowing that as long as he believes and repents his sins, he will be forgiven. It allows him to know that his life isn't over yet. He still has a chance to change and make the life he always wanted. He doesn't know how many more people he will need to see or how much more he needs to learn, but he's more ready than ever to take on this adventure and learn more. He never knew he'll ever be this excited to know God and see what's in store for him. He smiles and takes a deep breath, then steps through the threshold of the store. Walking into darkness and waiting for the wind to take him to some beautiful place.

The wind picks up and rushes past him. The whistles of the heavy breeze ring in his ears. He closes his eyes and thinks about the girl. The mystery girl who he longs to see how she fits into all this. *How old will she be next? It's been a de-aging process of five years so far. She looked ten this last time, so this next time she should be five. Maybe then I'll be able to see her face and have knowledge of who she is.* The wind picks him up as if he were a baby and carries him around the pitch-black room, twisting him around like a top and turning him all over the place. He listens to the wind and trusts the process as he knows he will be safe upon landing. He holds his arms out like he's enjoying every second and taking in every bit of what's happening.

He lands on his butt and realizes with every landing it has become more and more painful. *Maybe the pain is a good thing. I'm sure it's a form of punishment as well as for me to learn my lesson.* He opens his eyes and blinks as they've become blurred from holding them closed for too long. As his vision comes to, he sees a beautiful scene indeed. The majestic landscape and horizon. The sun shining bright and not a cloud in the sky. Birds flying around and one swoops past his head. He looks down and notices he's on top of a mountain, sitting on a ledge perfectly for him to see the beauty of the world.

A sharp pain throbs a few times from his behind. "Ow! My body is really starting to ache," he says as he directs that toward God.

"You think your body aches. Why don't you try being my age," a voice says from above.

"God?" Bryan questions.

"No, young man. Look above you."

Bryan looks up and sees an old man sitting on the ledge just upon him. "Mathew, I presume?"

"You're catching on, I presume." Mathew smirks. Mathew is an old man with a full head of white hair. His face is semiwrinkled but still has some youth to it. He's of light complexion like he doesn't tan in the sun. He's skinny and of average height. His lips are full and nose turned up a bit. His eyes are ice blue. He's wearing an old-style brown robe as if he came straight from the Bible. He has sandals on his feet. He is kicking them back and forth while peering out at the horizon with a look of relief.

"I'm Bryan."

He smirked again. "I know who you are, Bryan. We all know who you are. Would you just look at it? The world is a beautiful place." Bryan glances back out at the beauty and basks in the ambiance of the world itself. "If you look at it just right, you can almost see the curve, showing how round the world really is."

"Where are we, Mathew?"

"Probably my favorite place in the entire universe, besides heaven. We're at the top of Mount Sinai," Mathew answers with compassion.

"I think I've heard of it. Sounds familiar to me," Bryan says back.

Mathew begins to laugh a jolly laugh that makes Bryan think of Santa Claus. "I most certainly hope so, Bryan. If you picked up a Bible and read it, then you'd know for sure what I'm talking about."

Bryan grabs the back of his head like he was going to scratch an itch. "Yeah…I have been meaning to do that."

"Lying now, are we?"

"Okay, so I didn't intend to." Bryan chuckles. "I do now though. I've been learning so much, and the Bible now seems so interesting to me."

"Well, it should, Bryan. It's a bunch of true stories told over a long period of time. It's practically a history book they don't teach you in school. History that everyone should have some knowledge about."

"It seems to be full of wisdom we all can use on a daily basis," Bryan says while kicking his feet and staring at the sky.

"Indeed, it is. Wise men wrote it about even wiser men. Well, some weren't so wise. It also tells you what happens when you don't follow God or believe in him. It does have plenty of knowledge to help you and everyone else in this magnificent world grow. A mustard seed of knowledge is all we need to become faithful to the Lord," Mathew responds.

"That is a very wise saying. How long have you been here, Mathew?"

"Sounds like you know our whole spew now, don't you?" Mathew laughs.

"Took some time and help from a mystery girl, but I think I'm figuring it out.

"Well, I've been sitting here for six hundred and twenty-one years."

Bryan looks up at Mathew without hesitation. "That's a hell of a lot longer than the others were waiting."

"Hell? I don't know if hell should be involved. But yes, I was informed before everyone else. Sent here to wait," Mathew says back.

"Sorry, I shouldn't have said that."

Mathew laughs that jolly laugh again. "It's quite all right, Bryan. I've heard many things over my many, many years. You could say my ears are no longer virgin."

"I guess so, Mathew. Still, I apologize. Why would he make you wait for so long? He could've just sent you here today."

"There is no sense of time in our world. Where we live time is not a factor. Besides, this teaches patience and also allows us to listen to him. Follow his Word and trust his process. I'm dedicated to God and the Lord Jesus Christ. I'll do whatever he asks of me. Besides, I have eternity. What's a few hundred years to me," Mathew says with a half-smile.

"Very true, Mathew. What's heaven like?"

"Heaven? It's beautiful. It's majestic. It's everything you dream it would be. That's all I can say about that. You'll just have to find out for yourself one day."

Bryan nods his head and looks back out to the world beyond him, staring passionately and feeling glorified by the view. "It makes me feel so small."

"Sometimes we feel so small compared to how big the world is. Sometimes we feel insignificant like we don't matter." He opens his arms as if showing off a brand-new car. "No matter how small or insignificant we feel, you do matter. You matter to the world and to him, Bryan. As long as you believe you do."

"Belief sometimes is a hard thing to do," Bryan responds.

"Belief isn't hard. What's hard is knowing who you listen to. Satan likes to talk to people. Persuade them into doing what he wants. Sometimes it sounds like the right thing to do. That's his whole trick, the sly devil. There are four hundred and ten reasons why you shouldn't listen to him. Knowing who you're listening to is the first step and hardest. Once you reach that step, it becomes easier to weed out Satan and just listen to God himself. There are six hundred and thirteen reasons why you should listen to God."

"He likes to be called Lucifer."

Mathew huffs and shakes his head. "Lucifer was a name he had before all this. Before his tirade. He's the devil or Satan now. A fallen angel that wanted more than he was given."

"How come I never hear God?"

"That's because you aren't listening to him. He talks to you all the time, Bryan. Through the wind, through dreams, and even through other people. His work is very precise."

"I've ignored him my whole life," Bryan says while putting his hand in his face with shame.

"Don't feel ashamed, Bryan. Feel proud that you are getting to know him now. It's never too late to know God. He did all this for you so that you can know him and believe in him."

Bryan's eyes well up with tears. "I hear what you're saying, but I'm still not sure how to fully believe. Put my trust in him."

Mathew's voice begins to echo as it fades away. "Where there's a will, there's a way." Then he disappears into the air. Dark clouds begin to move in quickly. They cover the sky above Bryan and begin to swirl. They twirl and swirl downward toward him, lifting him as he is wrapped inside of it like a package on Christmas day. They carry him off the mountain and away.

Chapter 12

HE SPINS INSIDE the dark clouds as it carries him across the land. It feels as if it's traveling so fast with speeds that nobody has ever encountered before. Not even a rocket ship could keep up with it. Before he knows it, he is thrown from the cloud tornado and lands roughly into a flower patch. He grabs ahold of his body and rolls around in agony, moaning in pain. After a few seconds, he slowly sits up as the pain begins to subside.

"A flower patch. Reminds me of *The Wizard of Oz*. Hope these flowers don't make me fall asleep," he says aloud while rubbing his side. "Roses." He begins to breathe deeply with his nose, smelling the rose fragrance. It soothes him and makes him feel so calm. He looks out above the flowers from his sitting position and sees miles and miles of land—the patch of roses he is in and the rest is tall grass and wildflowers. He looks in all directions and even above him but doesn't see anyone. He's expecting another visitor.

I must be alone on this one? he questions in his head.

"You're not alone, Bryan," a voice says.

Bryan looks around intently. "How did you know what I thought?"

"God told me what to say and I said it," the voice responds.

Bryan continues to look around all over but sees nobody. "Where are you?"

"I'll be wherever you need me to be. With the grace of the Lord, I'll be the wind. With the power of God, I'll be the plants. For you, however, I'll be right here…to your left on the ground," the voice says.

Bryan looks to his left and down only to see another old gentleman lying on the ground with his hands behind his head, looking as if he's enjoying every aspect of life itself. Just relaxing and watching the clouds float by. He's clean-shaven and has a bald head with hair on the sides and back. His hair is pure white. His face looks wrinkled but still full of life. His eyes are green like grass. He has a large nose but not long, just wide. His skin is olive-colored. His eyebrows are a bushy white that matches his hair. He is short in stature and pudgy. He's wearing a brown robe just like Mathew and has matching brown sandals. "Who must you be?

"I'll be James, your final visitor. I'll be here for five hundred and fifteen days. I'm glad you've finally arrived," says James as if he already knew when Bryan would show up.

"I've learned a lot recently, James. How does a criminal like me who's done bad still become worthy of God? It has to be more than belief."

James sits up slowly with an old man grunt. "There are one hundred and fourteen roses around us now. Soon there will be one hundred and fifteen. Once you plant a flower, it will accumulate through pollination. The flowers help the bees. The bees in return help the flowers populate. T'is a cycle which shows everything is here and happens for a reason." Bryan pulls out his pad and begins writing all the numbers Mathew gave. Then he writes down the numbers James just gave him. "You could have forty-seven words on that pad and still be clueless until forty-eight." Bryan writes down those numbers as well. "Those be the numbers most important," James says.

"I know what you're saying, James. The flowers have faith that the bees will help them. Just as the bees have faith that the flowers are there for them," Bryan says back. "I should have faith that God will help me when things get dark, just as God has faith in me to be there with him."

"Precisely," James responds with enthusiasm. "You're not dumb like you think you are. You've been living in the shadow of Satan far too long. God can open your eyes to so many things. He can open your brain to even more."

Bryan ponders what James has told him. "You are very wise. No wonder that girl loves your story the most."

"She must have good taste and understanding of the Bible?"

"That she does. She is a smart little girl with a bright future. Well…if she has a future. I'm beginning to think she isn't real."

"Oh, she's real all right," James responds.

"Then she's a spirit like you, Mark, Luke, Mathew, and John?"

James giggles an old-man giggle. "No. Far from it. One day, she will do great things in this world. Be a savior of sorts. She will do God's work as he commands her to do." Bryan stares into James's eyes in confusion. "She's the spirit of someone real, Bryan. Her spirit was called upon to come and help guide you through this maze of a mall. A mall God created just for you. Your purgatory if you will. For God knew you wouldn't be able to do this alone. Nobody can do anything alone. Everyone needs help. Whether it be God's help or the help of others."

"Who is she? I feel like I know her, but I don't at the same time," Bryan asks.

"That will come in due time. You just have to listen and think hard. She's your guiding angel. Without her, your purpose is nothing."

"That sounds harsh," Bryan replies with an offended stance.

"May sound harsh, but it's true. Everyone has a different purpose in life. Some never figure their purpose out because they walk too close to the devil. Others do figure it out and in return make the world that much better. All purposes mean just as much as every other purpose."

"No purpose left behind," says Bryan jokingly.

"I wish that were true, but like I said, purposes are left behind sometimes. When the devil grabs ahold of people for life."

"This place is almost as beautiful as Mount Sanai. Where are we? What beautiful place of the Bible are we at now?" asks Bryan with his attention drawn deep into James's eyes.

"Place from the Bible?" James repeats what Bryan said to him.

"Yea, Luke and Mark were at a pyramid, which I know is in the Bible. Mathew was at Mount Sanai, which he said was in the Bible. Where are we now?"

James laughs hysterically at an old man. "I didn't know we had to be in places the Bible mentions."

Bryan looks upon James now with confusion. "I guess you're right. John was in the mall."

"We are where God wants us to be."

"Is this a real place?

James looked around at the beautiful flat land. "Well, I wish I could say we are in a beautiful place from the Bible to help inspire you more. Sadly, we are in Illinois, I believe."

"Illinois?"

James let out a huge laugh again. This time it was even bigger and louder than before. "Yes! Illinois!" he replies loudly.

"That's kind of a letdown, to be honest. I've never been to Illinois, but I didn't think God would bring me here."

"I didn't either until he did. God has a sense of humor. You may not have known that. He is probably laughing hard up there now."

Bryan smirks a bit. "Sense of humor, huh?"

"Yes!" James says with a smile. "A sense of humor. He probably thought, what a great joke to send you all over Egypt only for you to end up in Illinois." James giggles.

"I guess so." Bryan begins to laugh and the two laugh as they peer out at the flat meadow beyond. "You know, when I talked to him at the mall, he sounded very angry."

"Yes, well, He tends to do that. He wanted you to know how serious he was. Fire and brimstone is his thing. He wants only the best for you. After all, you are his son," James says.

"His son? Like Jesus?"

James laughs again. "You really are clueless about the Bible, Bryan. No not exactly like Jesus. You're not the Lord and Savior sent from heaven to take away all our sins. We all are his sons and daughters."

Bryan now looked like he had an epiphany. "Ahh. That's why he is the Father."

"Correct. See, you're not dumb, Bryan. You just need help like we all need help. He created the world and all of us in it. He's the Father, the Son, and the Holy Ghost. It completes the trinity."

"Is the son Jesus then?" Bryan asks with confidence.

"You could say that. God is all three in the Trinity. God the Father, God the Son, and God the Holy Ghost. Jesus is God the Son," James explains.

"So Jesus is God? I thought he was a different person."

"You could say that too. Jesus is God but a different form of God if you will. It's the trinity.

"This is all so confusing."

James responds, "Is it really though. Think about it."

Well, I guess it's not that confusing. God can be all three since he's God. God can take these forms and still be fully God.

"You're really using that brain now. God must be opening it up for you to understand all he wants you to understand," James says.

Bryan looks at James and smiles a sincere smile. "That may be, James, but I don't know if I can do it. Have faith and let him into my heart. The only one I've ever truly loved is Brenda." As the words leave his mouth, a whirlwind gusts upon them and lift Bryan. As he is twirling with it, he looks down and yells, "I need more answers! Don't take me yet!"

Then he hears James's voice echo toward him. "I know you will find a way to have faith, Bryan! After all, your daughter reads the Bible twice by age ten!" Bryan is then swooped away, unable to see where he is going.

Chapter 13

HE AWAKENS NEXT to the fountain with the angel centerpiece inside the mall. He sits up quickly and gets a head rush. "My daughter!" he shouts with a deep breath. *That girl said she read the Bible twice by age ten. That's what James said my daughter did too. She's my daughter. My sweet baby Brenda.*

He stands up with force and begins looking around for her. She is nowhere in sight. He rushes through the people, extending his arms to keep them at bay. He fully knows that they are more or less ghosts, but it's the thought that keeps his mind at ease, making sure he's not disturbed while he's on the search. He comes back to a stop in front of the fountain with the angel spitting water from her trumpet.

He stares blankly at the fountain, fully memorizing every curve and feature. The angel is a female with hair down to the middle of her back. She has on a robe that he imagines to be white—so white, it makes the snow look dull in comparison. She has a necklace on and jewels throughout her robe hanging from small chains that connect from shoulder straps to the bottoms of the robe. He imagines those all to be gold as well, but the jewels throughout he thinks of them as a mix of emeralds and sapphires. The robe cuts off at her knees and she is barefoot. One leg straight down holding her up. The other legs are brought back in an L. Almost like she's kissing someone for the first time and her foot rises back in a movie-style passion. Her hands both holding the trumpet to her mouth as her eyes are closed. The water flows from the front of the trumpet with one consistent flow. The statue itself is about five feet in height. She is standing on a pedestal in the middle of the huge water bowl. The centerpiece finishes the huge water bowl. He looks inside the water and sees no coins. No wishes people had thrown in just hoping they'd come true.

If I had just one coin right now, I'd throw it in and wish to see my daughter, he thinks as he randomly reaches into his pocket with the pad and pencil. To his amazement, he feels a coin under the pad, half of it in the pad under the paper. He pulls it out and sees a quarter between his fingers. He lets it slide down to his palm, and he stares at it for moments. He looks back at the fountain as his eyes flicker back and forth from the fountain and the coin in his palm. *I wish my daughter was here right now with me*, he thinks as he tosses the coin into the fountain.

As the coin hits the water and slowly floats to the bottom, the water starts to turn red. It looked like someone was bleeding heavily in the water. The water from the trumpet slowly comes to a stop like there is a clog in it now. The ground begins to shake with a rumble. The water in the bowl is now moving like the ocean, like someone tilted the bowl a bit. It waves back and forth from side to side. Small waves that a tiny surfer would love to just ride. The water begins flowing back out of the trumpet, and as it does, the water in the bowl begins to clear up. The rumble of the ground subsides, and the waves begin to calm. As the trumpet flows, the water becomes clear again, and eventually the red water from the trumpet becomes clear as well. He sees the coin now has disappeared from the bottom of the huge water bowl.

The chime goes off, and Bryan turns quickly and sharply to the direction it came from. The chime goes off again, but this time from the direction he was just looking at. He turns again just as quickly and sharply as before. His eyes are flicking all around, but he doesn't see Brenda. The chime went off a third time, but this time it sounded like it was now surrounding him. He can't tell the direction. He begins to spin as he flicks his eyes all around rapidly. In the process of spinning, he falls back onto his butt. The spinning has left him disoriented. He closes his eyes and tries to block out everything around him to help calm his nerves.

"Are you all right?" a little girl's voice says from behind him. He opens them quickly, still slightly disoriented. She comes around to his left and puts her hand on his shoulder. "Bryan?"

He peers up to her with his mouth open like he is seeing life for the first time. He grabs ahold of her hand that lies on his shoulder and holds it while looking into her bright blue eyes. She now looks like she's five years old, just like he suspected. He sees her long blonde hair, just perfectly straight and parted down the middle. Her hair is just as blonde as her mother's and just as thin as her hair too. She is smiling slightly but looks more concerned for Bryan. He sees a few freckles now throughout her face. Small, adorable freckles, mostly around her nose and cheeks. Not many to call her a freckle face but just enough to show character in her face. Her chin looks a lot like his dad when he was her age. Just like that, her face blurs back except for her eyes and lips.

"Bryan? Everything okay?" she asks once more.

He brings his smile back to a steady face he normally wears. "Yes. Sorry. I thought I had seen something for a minute. It's now gone." He lets go of her hand but regrets it instantly as the feel of her warm flesh makes him feel blissful. He brings himself up to his feet.

"I got that Bible that you asked for," Brenda says enthusiastically while holding out toward him.

"Brenda?" he questions with confusion.

"Yes? I told you that was my name before. Are you sure that you're okay?"

Bryan begins to tear up. "Oh my...I can't believe this whole time," he says then pauses to wipe tears from falling down his cheeks. "Your dad teaches you about the Bible?"

"Yes, he is. Right now, he is teaching me the Old Testament. I'm learning so much. I'm currently reading Exodus, but I plan on having the whole Bible read by the end of the year." She pauses then continues. "I can't wait to finish it. Dad said if I read for thirty minutes a day, I can have it done in six months."

"You're so beautiful, Brenda," he says with tears now just falling down his face uncontrollably. "Do you recognize me at all?"

"Of course, silly! You're Bryan. It's funny because that's my dad's name too!"

"He sounds like a great man," Bryan replies while now wiping the tears from his cheek again. "All right," he says as he perked up with determination. "I'm going to give you names and numbers and you give me the scripture."

"Let's do it!" she says eagerly.

"Mathew 6:13."

She flips through the book with many turns of the pages until she finds Mathew. She flips some more until she reaches chapter six. She uses her finger to scroll down to thirteen. "Okay, are you ready to write?"

Bryan giggles. "Yes, go ahead."

"And lead us not into temptation but deliver us from evil. For yours is the kingdom and the power and the glory, forever. Amen."

He writes it down just as she speaks the words. "Okay, now go back to four ten."

"Then Jesus said to him, be gone Satan; for it is written, you shall worship the Lord your God and him only shall you serve."

"Okay, good, baby girl. Now go back to six. I didn't see this one—6:21."

She flips a page to find 6:21. "For where your treasure is, there your heart will be also."

Bryan finishes writing that down. "Sounds like they all want me to believe fully unto God and only God." He now thinks to himself, *The last one seems to be talking about Brenda. She is my treasure, and I know my heart is with her.* He looks back up to Brenda's blurred-out face and stares directly into her eyes.

"What about that last one? Is God your treasure?" she asks.

"No, I don't believe he is. My treasure would be my daughter."

"I didn't know you had a daughter?"

Bryan gives a half-crescent smile from the side of his mouth. "Yes. She is a year and a half right now. Her name is Brenda."

"Just like mine!" Brenda said with exhilaration.

"Right!" he replies with just as much delight. "Go to Mark 12:30."

She flips the pages as if she knows exactly where to go. She finds Mark and flips until she reaches chapter twelve. "Okay, right here!" she says thrilled to keep going. "And you shall love the Lord your

God with all your heart and with all your soul and with all your mind and with all your strength."

He writes it down. "Luke now. Luke 6:37."

She flips more pages quickly, trying to get to Luke with no time wasted. "Okay, here it is. 'Judge not, and you will not be judged; condemn not, and you will not be condemned; forgive, and you will be forgiven.' That one sounds really good. We are not judges or condemners. As we forgive then he will forgive us."

"That makes perfect sense, Brenda," he says as he finishes up the passage on his pad.

"Do John 1:4 next," he demands.

She sticks her tongue slightly out through her lips as she turns the pages to John. "First page of John," she said while feeling accomplished. "In him was life, and the life was the light of men."

"Interesting. That one was short," Bryan says with a laugh of relief. "John 3:15."

With a flip of the page, she finds it. "That whoever believes in him may have eternal life."

"Good another short one. My hand is slightly tired at this point. The last one is James. James 1:14."

"Okay," she replies while flipping toward the back of the New Testament. "But each person is tempted when he is lured and enticed by his own desire."

"Okay, now do the next one, 1:15."

Brenda continues, "Then desire when it has conceived gives birth to sin, and sin when it is fully grown brings forth death."

"So that one is saying not to desire things because desire brings sin. It's sinful to desire," Bryan informs Brenda knowing she understood it before him. "4:7 now."

Brenda, with her tongue out again, turns the pages to chapter four. "Submit yourselves therefore to God. Resist the devil, and he will flee from you."

"Now 4:8."

"Draw near to God, and he will draw near to you. Cleanse your hands, you sinners, and purify your hearts, you double-minded."

"Last one, 5:15."

She looks to the second page opened and sees it's right there. "And the prayer of faith will save the one who is sick, and the Lord will raise him up. And if he has committed sins, he will be forgiven."

"Okay, so James said that 4:7–8 were the most important ones. Basically, they say to be with God. Stay away from the devil and ask forgiveness to be purified."

"They all seem to be about asking forgiveness and giving your belief in God. They really want to pound that into your head, huh?" Brenda answers.

"Yes, they do. It's something I've lacked in life."

"So put your faith in him and you'll be saved. Die for him and you'll be saved. Don't be selfish in your ways because selfishness is sin and that brings the devil," Brenda says.

"It still doesn't explain how I get out of here. How I can get back to my life and use what I've learned," Bryan replies.

"Well, your job is obviously not done yet. You know, I really love what James had to say, Dad."

"He will be your favorite, I'm sure..." Bryan pauses and then replies, "What did you just call me?"

"Dad? That's what I always call you," she says as his eyes well up with tears once again. He can't help but cry as his emotions are triggered and his heart longs for her to recognize him as her father. "You are my dad, aren't you?"

"Yes, yes, I am. I'm glad you finally see that, Brenda, baby," he says back while putting his fingers to his eyes.

"Why are you crying?"

"I'm just so happy right now. They are tears of happiness, sweetheart."

She gives him a big hug, and they hold each other for what seems like an eternity. As they let go, he glances up at her face and sees it's now fully shown once again. He can see every aspect of her face. Every curve and feature. This was the happiest moment of his entire life. It makes up for not being there for her birth as he feels he has witnessed a rebirth. Not just his own but hers as well.

Chapter 14

THEY START TO hear a disturbance from the crowd. The sound of hooves clapping against the hard tile flooring. They seem to be drawing near to them with every clap. The faster they clap, the louder it sounds.

"Bryan!" an evil voice yells. "Bryan Butler!" the voice shouts again. The crowd of people moves out of the way as if someone with magic used a force push to slide them aside. Bryan sees Satan now lurching toward him. Satan points his long red finger with his long black nail at Bryan while continuing his steps of determination. "Bryan! We have unfinished business!"

Satan now looks bigger than he was, reaching about seven feet in height, and has more muscle than before. He looks as if he is pumping iron steadily since the last time they spoke. "Get behind me, baby girl," Bryan says to Brenda as he pushes her behind him to guard her from the evil approaching.

Satan reaches Bryan and gets face to chest with him. Satan peers down at Bryan with fire in his eyes. "You owe me your soul!" His voice is as deep and loud as any voice can possibly get.

"I don't owe you a thing, Satan," Bryan calmly says back.

"Really?" Satan responds with even more fire. "You crashed my ceiling, and I gave you a cookie after that! I was nothing but generous, and you think you don't owe me a thing!"

"Because of that, I owe you my soul?" Bryan questions.

"You owe me your soul because you said I could have it if I helped you!"

"But you didn't help me. I told you I didn't want your help, Satan."

Satan grows a tad bigger and redder than before. "Quit calling me, Satan! My name is Lucifer!"

Bryan stands tall with confidence. "Your name is Satan. You lost the right to Lucifer when you rebelled against God."

Satan looks up with his hands to the sky and screams a loud bloodcurdling scream. "Your soul is supposed to be mine!"

"No. It's for God. It's for heaven. Not for the likes of you," Bryan replies. Brenda is peeking out now from behind Bryan, shaking in fear of the monster in front of them. "I owe you nothing."

"I made all this for you! I made it all so you could give me what is owed! This has all been me. I'm in control!"

"I'm in control, Satan. God is in control. You have no influence on me any longer. Be gone and go back to where you came," demands Bryan. "You didn't make this, you liar. God made this just for me. He sits at the top of the twelfth floor."

"God! God doesn't do this! God can't control me! I will do as I please!" Satan replies.

"You may do what you please but so do I. I choose who I follow and who I believe in. You don't choose for me."

Satan screams once again, this time so loud it rattles the whole building. Bryan, however, shows no fear or sign of backing down. He knows deep down God won't allow Satan to hurt him as long as he doesn't allow it. "You think you're so smart now, don't you, Bryan! Wise beyond your years! You think you're just like Jesus!"

"Nobody can be just like Jesus. I do, however, think I'm stronger than you are." Bryan smiles a passionate smile. "I have the power of God on my side."

"God fears me! Why do you think he shunned me to hell and earth! He didn't want me in heaven because he knew I could overthrow him!"

"I don't believe that, and I don't think you believe it either. God got rid of you because you were a nuisance. You were a pathetic excuse for an angel. He sent you to hell because that's what you deserve. He allows you to run earth because he wants his people to choose right from wrong. He gives us the decision to follow him or listen to the likes of you. It's called free will. Anyone smart enough will know that you're a liar. That you're manipulative. That you're too sly and evil to listen to and shun you with every part of their being. You're not wanted here nor are you wanted anywhere. The only people who want you are the weak-minded fools that think you're God."

"I am God! I became a God when he sent me to hell! The lord of darkness! God of hell!"

"You're no god. God is the God of Hell. He just lets you run it. He lets you run it because you're no better than the poor soul sent there."

Satan screams again and backs up from Bryan. He extends his left arm and spreads his fingers. Instantly, Brenda is dragged out, screaming from behind Bryan, and slides to Satan. Bryan tries to grab her hand but fails to hold on. "Help me, Dad!" Brenda cries.

"Hold tight, baby, I will save you."

"You won't do a thing, Bryan! You don't have the power I have!" Satan screams with a smirk on his ugly bull face. "You're soul for hers!" he demands.

Bryan hesitates and stops instantly from pursuing. Bryan looks down at Brenda with concern written all over his face. He sees the fear in her eyes. Fear filled with hope that her father would save her. *I'm supposed to protect her. How could I let him get her?* he thought as he glared back down to her. He sees tears water up her left eye and roll down her cheek. It hits her chin and falls to the floor. His meaty red hand and long fingers gripping tight around her wrist. He notices that her skin is reddening around where his hand forcibly grasps it. She tries so hard to break his grip but to no avail. She pulls and tugs and even kicks his bull leg, but Satan doesn't let up.

"I feel something strong in this one!" Satan yells with an evil smile. "Feels like something I've only felt in one other person! Maybe I should take her soul!"

Bryan brings his eyebrows down in anger and glares back up to Satan. He begins to breathe heavily, huffing and puffing like he's a defensive lineman ready to take on the quarterback. *I've got to face this without fear. I've got to break this grip and take Satan out of the picture. Nobody messes with my little Brenda.* Bryan begins to show his teeth as he gets angrier and fiercer.

"Looks like Daddy isn't going to do a thing, little girl!" Satan hollers at Brenda.

She screams back at him without fear. "You underestimate him. He's strong and fearless. He will save me. I believe in him."

Satan laughs hard and loudly. "He's weak!"

Bryan continues to think, but now it's how he is going to prevent Satan from taking Brenda's soul. "Sacrifice," an ominous voice says that only Bryan could hear.

Sacrifice? I must sacrifice myself to save her. Whoever would save his life shall lose it, but whoever loses his life for my sake will save it. I must sacrifice myself to save Brenda. Satan feels something in her. James said she would be a savior of some sort. That she will do great things at the command of God. Therefore, me sacrificing myself for her is the same as doing it for God. Sacrifice.

The ominous voice says once again as Bryan says *sacrifice* in his head, "Sacrifice."

Bryan raises his eyebrows and looks a lot calmer now. "Okay, Satan, you win," he speaks. "Let her go, and I'll come to you."

Satan chuckles and loosens his grip on Brenda's arm but doesn't let go yet. "How do I know this isn't a trick!"

"It's not. You let her go, and I'll come your way. Trust me, I'm no longer a liar."

Satan laughs and lets go of Brenda's arm fully. Her arm is red and slightly bruised from the strong grip he held. She scurries away holding her arm and goes to Bryan. She wraps her arms around him and squeezes tight. Bryan puts an arm around her and leans down, giving her a kiss on the top of her head. "You'll be safe now, baby. I'm going to do what I have to now. Stay here."

Bryan lets go of Brenda and walks past her. He slowly makes his way toward Satan, while Satan begins to smile more and more. "Yes!" Satan shouts. "Yes!"

Bryan reaches within the grasp of Satan and stops momentarily. He looks up to Satan's eyes, which seem so high up. He said out loud with determination and conviction, "I will lose my life for her sake."

After letting that out, he charges Satan with every bit of strength he has. He grabs Satan wrapping his arms around him, pushing Satan back. Satan grabs back with his hands on Bryan's shoulders. Bryan continues to push, and Satan tries to stop him, sliding back. He slides all the way to the railing of the second floor. Bryan looks down and sees the first floor below them. Satan tries to push back once again but is unable to move Bryan. Bryan closes his eyes and pushes as hard as he can with one final thrust. Satan rolls over the rail but keeps a hold of Bryan and takes him with him. Both of them head over and fall to the first floor with great velocity.

Chapter 15

BRYAN OPENS HIS eyes and looks around. He notices he is back in his cell—back in this jail, back to his reality. He jumps off of his mat scared of what happened with Brenda. He is breathing heavily and is worried sick to his stomach. Now he's back, and everything he has learned can be put to good use. The Word of God is strong, and his faith now running its course.

Bryan steps to the cell bars and grabs ahold of them. He pictures Kara standing on the other side, holding little Brenda, looking at him as if he were a failure. He realizes he's not a failure though. This is all a part of the plan. The plan God made for him. God wants him to get better. God wants him to see all his errors and wants to change himself. God wants him to see what all he had to live for.

It's my time now. My time to face my music. I know in my heart that I will be out of here soon enough. I know in my heart that God is by my side. As long as I stay faithful and live life unselfishly, he will provide me with what I need. My Brenda. Now I wait for everything to play out so that I can be with her once again. So I can teach her about God, Jesus, and the Bible. I'm ready, Lord. I'm ready to walk this path of light you've laid in front of me. Satan tempts me no longer. Brenda will grow into the woman she's supposed to be. She will walk with you as well and do as you command. I'll make sure of that. If all that I've seen is true, then it will happen.

"Butler!" a voice shouts and breaks Bryan's concentration. Bryan blinks and looks over to the corrections officer standing by the door. "Damn, Butler, are you okay? You look like you've seen a ghost."

Bryan smiles. "Yes, I'm better than okay, officer. I'm seeing things from a new perspective. I guess in the process I zoned out."

"Well, okay then. Do you want lunch?"

Bryan smiles bigger. "I'd love some lunch. Feels like forever since I've eaten anything but chocolate."

The corrections officer stares blankly at Bryan. "You don't have any chocolate." Then he walks in and looks toward the toilet.

Bryan laughs hysterically. "Don't look in there. I didn't mean chocolate. I meant to say breakfast."

The officer raises an eyebrow and shrugs. "Okay, then. It's only been four hours." Then he peers back over to the toilet. "You sure you weren't eating anything you had mistaken for chocolate?"

"No. I'm sure, officer."

The correction officer walks out of the door and comes back with a tray. "Lunch?"

Bryan nods his head yes and grabs the tray that is being passed through the hole in the bars. "Thank you."

The officer nods and smiles then goes to walk out. "Hey, officer."

The correction officer stops mid-stride and turns a bit toward Bryan. "Yes?"

"Do you think I can go to the library later? I'd like to check out a Bible."

The officer sighs. "You know it's not library day, Butler."

"Yes, I know. I just thought you could make an acceptation just this once," Bryan says politely.

The officer sighs once more and looks at his watch. "All right, let me tell you what. After I get done serving lunch, I'll come back and get you."

"Thank you, officer," Bryan said ecstatically.

"Don't mention it. Just be ready when I come back. Make it fast so nobody else sees. The last thing I need is a bunch of inmates crying because you got to go and they didn't."

"I'll be ready, sir."

"I'm only doing this because I'm a God-fearing man. Seeing someone ask for a Bible warms my heart a bit. Besides, I think a Bible would do you some good." The officer turns back and walks out of the door.

Bryan sets his tray down on his cot hanging out of the side of the wall and sits down next to it. As he sits there thinking about his future and about Brenda, he feels something strange in his pocket. He digs his hand in and feels two golf balls. *The golf balls!* he thinks with excitement. He pulls them out and sees one white and one yellow. They're the exact same ones he picked up from the nice men in his dream. "This is weird?" he says out loud. *It makes me feel like I'm still dreaming. Now I know it wasn't a dream. It was something far greater. These two golf balls stayed with me the whole time, and I forgot I had them.* He then remembers that when he picked them up, he couldn't read the monogram on the golf balls. He turns them over and now sees what they truly say. On the white ball, it reads Revelation. The yellow ball reads 22:21. *I don't know what this means, but I will soon enough. From here on, I'm in the Lord's hands now.* Then he says again, but this time out loud, "I'm in the Lord's hands now. Amen."

About the Author

DANNY HILL has lived in Ohio all his life. He has three dogs and many cats. He loves animals, nature, and helping others. He struggled for a long time with addiction, but that struggle led him to God. In return, God led him to his passion as a child, writing. He was able to focus on his writing and finally achieved a goal that had long eluded him. He's grateful for God and the Lord Jesus Christ. Without them, this wouldn't be possible for him.